HAMLET
Sports Special

Soccer

HAMLET
Sports Special

Soccer

Hamlyn
London · New York · Sydney · Toronto

The photographs on the cover and preliminary pages are:
Front cover Mariner of England and Aitken of Scotland battle for the ball during the home international championship
Back cover Pike and Allen with the FA Cup after West Ham United's win in 1980
Half-title page McQueen of Manchester United and Palmer of Manchester City in a soccer ballet
Title spread Maradona, the new sensation of the 1980s, beating Kaltz in the Copa de Oro tournament in Uruguay, 1981
Introduction page Morley, Aston Villa's winger, with Spurs' defender Perryman

This book was commissioned by 'Hamlet' Cigars

'Hamlet' and 'Benson and Hedges' are registered trade marks in the United Kingdom of J. R. Freeman & Son Limited and Benson & Hedges Limited respectively; both companies are subsidiaries of Gallaher Limited

Acknowledgements

The pictures in this book were obtained from the following sources:
All-Sport/Duncan Raban: back cover, title spread, 7; Ardea, London: 10; Associated Newspapers Limited: 40; BBC Hulton Picture Library: 11, 15, 59 (top), 93; Central Press, London: 60, 65 (top), 81; Colorsport: front cover, half-title, 14 (bottom), 17, 19, 21, 22, 25, 26, 27 (bottom), 31 (bottom), 32, 33, 34 (top), 35, 36 (top and bottom), 37, 38, 39 (left and right), 41 (top and bottom), 42, 43 (top and bottom), 44, 45, 46 (bottom), 47 (bottom), 49, 51, 61, 62 (top and bottom), 63 (top, centre and bottom), 64 (top and centre), 66 (top and bottom), 67 (top and bottom), 71 (top and bottom), 73 (bottom), 74, 75 (top, centre and bottom), 85 (bottom), 86, 87 (top and bottom), 88, 90 (top), 91 (top and bottom), 95 (top and bottom); Mary Evans Picture Library: 9, 13 (top and bottom), 14 (top right); Hamlyn Group Picture Library: 55 (bottom), 57, 59 (bottom); Hungarian News and Information Service: 79; Interfoto MTI, Hungary: 48; Keystone Press Agency: 24, 50, 52 (top), 55 (top), 69 (top and centre), 72 (bottom), 77 (top, centre and bottom), 78, 80 (top and bottom), 82 (top and bottom), 83 (top), 85 (top); Press Association: 14 (top left), 64 (bottom); Sporting Pictures (UK) Limited: 23, 27 (top), 31 (top), 34 (bottom), 46 (top), 47 (top), 90 (centre), 94 (top and bottom); Syndication International: 20, 29, 52 (bottom), 54, 56, 65 (bottom), 69 (bottom), 72 (top), 73 (top), 83 (bottom), 84, 90 (bottom)

Published 1981 by
The Hamlyn Publishing Group Limited
London · New York · Sydney · Toronto
Astronaut House, Feltham, Middlesex, England

ISBN 0 600 34663 3

Printed in Great Britain

Contents

Introduction

Benny Green

I cannot remember exactly when I first knew about football. Or to put it another way, I cannot remember a time when I did not know about it. I was seven years old when my father took me to my first match, Arsenal against Derby County, the last match of the 1934-35 season. But by the time I arrived on the Highbury terraces on that long-lost afternoon, I was already the custodian of professional knowledge. I knew the initials before the name of Hapgood, prince of footballers, stood for Edris Albert; I knew the difference between the Throstles and Hatters; I knew who played at Ayresome Park and who at Burnden Park; I knew which were the smallest and largest grounds in the First Division; I had conned by rote the line-up of the winning Arsenal cup side of 1930; I knew which were the eleven London clubs; I could recite the names of the twenty-two First Division clubs in alphabetical order. I knew the record transfer fees, number of goals in a season, number of caps in a career, number of Wembley final appearances. Football was my religion, Highbury my church, Hapgood, James and company the high priests nurturing a beautiful and romantic tradition.

Where did I acquire all this knowledge? Partly from my father, who encouraged my interest, and grew into the habit of passing on to me each week his edition of the *Racing and Football Outlook*; partly from his younger brother, my favourite uncle, who passed on to me his suede shinpads with the advice that before hitting a shot along the ground, the head had to be over the ball. (It was the nearest thing to a moral precept he ever imbibed, but it was more than enough to make him a sage and an honourable man in my eyes.) I picked it up partly from the boys at school, who were as potty about the game as I was. But I suspect most of all I picked it up from the air I breathed. Football was part of the atmosphere of our back streets, and a small boy could no more avoid it than he could sidestep the weather.

As Kipling says, we have only one virginity to lose, and where we lost it, there our hearts will be. That is why for me the modern jibber-jabber about sweepers and centre backs, about strikers and hit-men, is no more than the crackling of thorns under a pot. For me it will always be centre-halves and centre-forwards. That is the way it always was and ever will be, world without end, and so on. This apparent conservatism is not half as conservative as it sounds, because if you drop the trendy jargon, it soon becomes apparent that the English game has not changed all that much since I was an innocent. Less ball-players than there used to be, less wingers, more thuggery both on and off the field, more hairdressing appointments for the famous players, much semi-literate gobble-degook mouthed by self-important managers. Barrow and Gateshead vanished from the League usurped by Wimbledon and Wigan. But none of this is so fundamental it might not all be reversed in time.

No matter what the charlatans may say to the contrary, football is basically a simple game, which is why its appeal has proved universal. People who laugh at the ancient pretensions of the British Empire regarding the conquest of the globe should stop laughing and realise that the British pulled it off after all. Not with armies or statesmen, but with Bob Crompton and Arthur Grimsdell, with Dixie Dean and Tommy Walker, and, of course, with the twin geniuses of my boyhood, Eddie Hapgood and Alec James. If the rest of the world has caught up with us at last, and perhaps even passed us, that is no more than proof of the irresistible power and fascination of the game the British invented, perfected and deployed as a harmless way of colonising the entire planet.

History of Soccer
John Moynihan

Modern soccer is a global virus, the communal passion of countries, communities and races. Hence the wild nationalistic fervour which greeted Argentina's World Cup win against Holland in Buenos Aires in 1978. Any stranger who witnessed the wild rejoicing in their urban streets afterwards would have been left in no doubt about the incredible magnetism this comparatively simple game inspires.

And, yet, as the time machine chugs back through the ages of history, the popularity of soccer can be regarded as fairly recent, inspired at first by persevering football missionaries from Britain to continents like South America in the 1880s, and nearly a century later, by major television coverage of World Cup matches attracting millions of viewers. The ancient game was very different, secluded, mysterious, localised, and subject to very different rules.

When FIFA readmitted the People's Republic of China in 1979 after a long absence of thirty years, the largest football association in the world, with 150 members, welcomed back a country whose forebears back in the myths of time were responsible for originating a game of footer now known as soccer.

Not the modern game as we know it, which is justifiably claimed to have its origins at English public schools in the mid-nineteenth century – but a hearty recreation called Tsu Chu first played in 206 BC on the emperor's birthday during the Han Dynasty. A contemporary historian recorded the art: "Tsu must kick ... Chu is stuffed leather ball."

The emperor, Che'eng Ti was an enthusiastic player, but he and his courtiers also enjoyed being spectators at games played alongside the royal pavilion, unobstructed by brigands, hooligans or other unwelcome infiltrators.

The goals were tall compared with today's minute cages, consisting of two 30-ft high bamboo posts with silken goal rigging exquisitely attached. But the widths were narrow, only a yard wide. The rules were simple, the two teams being required to hoof a ball made of horsehair between their opponents' posts. For the losers, there were no suspensions, fines, or red and yellow cards, simply decapitations, or brisk floggings depending on the emperor's mood. For the winners, a sumptuous feast. A subsequent emperor was so touchy about the joys of Tsu Chu being criticised that he had the offender executed on the spot. The game was duly noted by foreign diplomats – and may well have been copied by countries at the other end of the Han camel trails.

The thunder of horsehair combat induced at least one Chinese poet, Li-Yu, to pen Tsu Chu in verse, and so create one of history's first footer poems:

A round ball and an oblong space with
two teams standing opposed
The ball flies across the moon at
the full
Captains are appointed and take their
places in accordance with regulation
unchanging
In the game make no allowance for kith and
kin and let not your mind be swayed
by partialities
Be cool, determined and show not the
slightest irritation when you fail . . .

Tsu Chu flourished in China until AD 25 – then other forms of ancient footer began to originate – and can be traced back in historical records to Japan, Greece, ancient Rome, Brittany and Normandy. The Normans with their special game of soule may well have first introduced the game to British shores when William the Conqueror invaded in 1066.

By medieval times, the noble art created by the Chinese had become a rough and tumble in Britain, played violently, and sometimes to the death, between towns, hamlets and manors. Instead of a football, horsehair, leather, or otherwise, a hog's

DRIBBLING

WELL KICKED

SOFT FALLING, FORTUNATELY

HOWS THAT UMPIRE

WELL DONE MAC!!

head was often used to inspire the fracas, played by every fit man available in the region. Football was especially popular on feast days like Shrove Tuesday. In Chester, the drapers took on the shoemakers in annual games.

But such roughhouses were not so popular with English monarchs. Edward II, Edward III and Henry IV all frowned upon the game because it was a rough distraction from archery practice. Romantic poets, perhaps from undercover presses, thought differently. One wrote:

And nowe in the winter, when men kill the fat swine
They get the bladder and blow it great and thin,
With many beans and peason put within:
It ratleth, soundeth, and shineth clere and fayre

While it is throwen and caste up in the ayre,
Each one contendeth and hath a great delite
With foote and with hands the bladder for to smile;
If it fail to grounde, they lifte it up agayne,
But this waye to labour they count it no payne . . .

That football flourished despite bans set down by the establishment can be seen from ancient English illustrations, like the two sweaty players shown in a misericord in Gloucester Cathedral. Subsequent kings found the game offended their cultures and James I ordered the kicking of a round ball to be a crime against the nation: "From this court I debarre all rough and violent exercises, as the foot-ball, meeter for lameing than making able the users thereof." It was James's grandson, Charles II, who encouraged the playing of footer, which

The first international, Scotland versus England at Glasgow in 1872. It resulted in a 0-0 draw.

like other sports and games had been banned by the Puritans.

The King's interest in the game was kindled by Count Albemarle who had returned from Florence after watching a local game of calcio. This resplendent game, started by the boom of a cannon, was played by two teams in ceremonial dress at the Olympic Stadium, Rome, before the opening match of the 1980 European Championships. It was easy to see why the noble Count had been hooked by the spectacle despite the rough handling. He sped back to tell Charles – and arranged a match between the King's team and his own. Albemarle's team claimed an away win, and King Charles had his merriness sapped by losing ten gold coins. But this game of footer gave him so much satisfaction that he had the royal ban on the game annulled.

Now the game moved towards its eventual emancipation, slowly at first, and still roughshod, as urchins booted leather around the expanding urban streets of the kingdom. For a time it went out of fashion

after the Stuarts, recorded unkindly by Joseph Strutt, a leading author, in 1801. In 'The Sports and Pastimes of the People of England', Strutt observed that "football was formerly much in vogue among the common people of England, though of late years it seems to have fallen into disrepute and is but little practised." Strutt blamed this on a hazard to limbs but with the Napoleonic wars in progress, young Englishmen were forever being press-ganged to do their duty on land and sea. Not much time for playing with round leather – and if there was, it had to be done in clogs because coins were scarce.

Football matches involving the aristocracy continued to flourish and one match in 1815 in Scotland between Selkirk and Yarrow, attended by all the local gentry, inspired Sir Walter Scott to add his own report in verse in the *Edinburgh Journal*:

From the brown nest of Newark its summons extending,
Our signal is waving in smoke and in flame;
And each forester blithe from his mountain descending

A hand-painted engraving of soldiers playing football by the nineteenth century English artist George Cruikshank.

*Bounds light o'er the heather to join in
the game.
Then strip lads and to it, though sharp be
the weather,
And if, by mischance, you should happen
to fall,
There are worse things in life than a tumble
on heather,
And life is itself but a game of football.*

Sir Walter's poem beckoned the arrival of the modern game and the drawing up of the Rules. After the Napoleonic Wars, young bucks at English public schools like Charterhouse, Winchester, Westminster, Eton and Harrow began inventing their own forms of footer – as a release from their own rigid and harsh environments.

The pupils of Westminster and Charterhouse were noble pioneers, creating the dribbling game which replaced the hacking and butch fighting which had powered on before. Undergraduates at Cambridge University also took up the game and the Cambridge rules were first drawn up there in 1848.

In the 1860s, football spread its wings to the North of England among working class teams. Sheffield, the oldest soccer club still in existence, had been founded in 1855, and seven years later, Notts County, the oldest Football League club, was formed,

two years ahead of neighbours Forest. Soccer milestones then began to pepper the years up to the end of the century.

A memorable event occurred at the Freemasons Tavern in Great Queen Street on a gaslit night in December 1863 when the English Football Association was founded. A split between the assembly resulted in F W Campbell and members of the Blackheath Club arguing about the new adoption of the Cambridge Rules. Campbell and his handling friends went their own way – the Rugby Union was formed eight years later.

Thus the game of soccer in England became more or less official, with C W Alcock, a muscular Old Harrovian, proving an able and enthusiastic secretary of the FA. It was Alcock who launched the FA Cup competition with the words "It is desirable that a Challenge Cup should be established in connection with the Association for which all clubs belonging to the Association should be invited to compete". The first final took place at Kennington Oval in 1872 when the Wanderers beat the Royal Engineers 1-0 in front of a crowd of 2,000. The famous competition which during the next century would regularly draw 100,000 spectators to Wembley for the greatest annual English sport-

11

ing occasion of the year, was duly under way.

The FA, who had originally drawn up their own set of rules in 1863 which made handling an overall offence, now began to move the game towards its modern counterpart. In 1865, tapes were first used as crossbars, and a year later, the offside rule was altered to allow a player to be onside when three of the opposing team were nearer their own goal line. In 1869, goal kicks were introduced. It was not until 1874 that umpires were first mentioned in the laws. In 1878, referees, who were arbitrators for linesmen, used whistles for the first time. Crossbars replaced tapes in 1875.

The game began to flourish around the British Isles with the formation of the Scottish, Welsh and Irish Football Associations, and the first official international between Scotland and England took place in 1872 at Glasgow in a match which ended in a goalless draw. The Scots, some of whom played for the first club formed north of the border in 1867, impressed with their clever passing skills in contrast to the overall dribbling tactics employed by the English.

The 1880s saw the beginnings of modern soccer. Again Alcock was a pioneer in helping to legalise professionalism in 1885, following a period of undercover payments between clubs and players in the North. After professionalism was adopted, players, especially Scotsmen, from austere cities like Glasgow, were quick to sign on; Suter and Love being the first as representatives of Darwen in Lancashire. The emergence of leading professional teams like Preston North End (the first team to win both the Football League Championship and the FA Cup in 1889), Blackburn Rovers and Aston Villa, dovetailed with the founding of the Football League in 1888.

The brainchild of William McGregor, a Birmingham draper, the League allowed itself only twelve founder members despite numerous applications. The twelve teams who would compete for the new title, some of them subsequently world famous club sides, were Accrington, Aston Villa, Blackburn Rovers, Bolton Wanderers, Barnsley, Derby County, Everton, Notts County, Preston North End, Stoke, West Bromwich Albion and Wolverhampton Wanderers. All were professional sides.

Ironically, the League, as was to happen more than once in later decades, were slow to make up their minds on a vital issue. It was not until November that they drew up their finalised points system with one point for a draw and two for a win. This was to endure the test of time right up to 1981, when at an emergency League meeting attended by representatives of 92 clubs, it was decided to award three points for a win.

Of the twelve teams elected, only Accrington failed to flourish under the new challenge – although they did not drop out of the League until 1962 under the name of Accrington Stanley because of financial troubles. Some of the other teams like Preston and Aston Villa gobbled up trophies as soccer moved imperiously into the 1900s. The laws meanwhile were still being advanced, with goal nets being used in an FA Cup Final for the first time in 1892. Floodlighting was experimented with – but the first League match under lights did not take place until the Portsmouth-Newcastle game in February 1956. Referees and linesmen replaced umpires in 1891. A red-faced FA had to accept the theft of the FA Cup from the window of a Birmingham shop in 1895. It was never recovered.

The Football League had increased their membership in 1893 by forming a Second Division – by 1905, there were 20 teams playing in two Divisions. New stadiums emerged, crowds increased, football fans came down from the North in carts and even riding horseback; 110,820 spec-

From the Sporting and Dramatic News *, an impression of England playing Scotland at the Oval, 1875. Note the player wearing a monocle.*

tators flooded the banks of Crystal Palace for the 1901 Cup Final between Tottenham Hotspur and Sheffield United. There had never been a crowd like this before for a football match.

Subsequently, the Football League moved cautiously with new policies. In 1919, two clubs were added to the two Divisions. One of them was Arsenal: they have never been out of the First Division since. A year later, a Third Division consisting of 22 clubs came into being, and in 1921, this league became the Third Division (South) to allow a Northern League to have a kick.

After another large gap in time the bottom halves of the two Third Divisions were formed into a Fourth Division in 1957-58. It was not until 1981 when attendances were falling, and a general crisis surrounded England's ailing domestic football, that the Football League really came out of their shell with a number of positive points voted in by their members. They were: three points for a win, no official (director or secretary) to be in-

Soccer at the universities. Cambridge playing Oxford on Parker's Piece in 1887. The playing area is marked by flags. An illustration from the Graphic *.*

13

Some famous soccer faces.
Right *Charles Alcock,
FA Secretary who thought
up the FA Cup
competition and the first
international match.* Far
right *Alf Common,
whose transfer from
Sunderland to
Middlesbrough in 1905
for £1,000 (the first
four-figure fee) caused an
FA investigation.*

*Herbert Chapman, the
first man to achieve wide
fame as a soccer manager,
managed both
Huddersfield and
Arsenal, the only two
clubs to achieve a hat-
trick of Championships.*

volved in the management or administration of more than one club, a transfer embargo on clubs with payments outstanding from other deals, and a gentlemen's agreement not to hire another League club's manager during the season. This was certainly a step forward by the League after decades of indecision and negative football decreed by worried, nervous managers trying to avoid the fate of so many of their company – the sack. Of all the employments available in the twentieth century to an Englishman, the post of football manager must have been as unenviable as an infantryman's in the front line.

But despite the high rate of sackings, great managers did appear in British soccer, including Herbert Chapman, who built up two winning sides, Huddersfield and Arsenal, between the two World Wars; Matt Busby, the canny Scot, who took over Manchester United at the end of the Second World War and created three splendid teams, one of which, the 'Busby Babes', were to perish in the 1958 Munich air crash; Stan Cullis, the former England centre half, and Wolves manager of that supremely fit side in the 1940s and 1950s; Sir Alf Ramsey, England's World Cup supremo in 1966; Bill Nicholson, master of the legendary Spurs double side in 1961; and the two governors of Liverpool, Bill Shankly and Bob Paisley, who both achieved mammoth prizes at Anfield.

And last, but not least, Jock Stein, Celtic, later Scotland's manager, and Brian Clough, rarely out of the headlines in the 1970s and 1980s for his extraordinary success in company with Peter Taylor in

raising two fading sides, Derby County and Nottingham Forest, into class teams capable of winning the Football League Championship and, in Forest's case, the European Cup, twice.

From the start of the twentieth century, soccer became a case of England against the Rest. The blinkered 'old guard' of the Football Association refused to accept that countries east of Dover were taking a healthy interest in booting a round ball around.

A Football Association touring team visited Germany in 1900. But when FIFA (the Federation of International Football Associations) was founded in Paris in 1904, the founder members included France, Belgium, Holland, Switzerland, Denmark, Sweden, but not England, Wales, Scotland and Ireland however, who all turned down the offer to join until two years later.

English domestic football was by now thriving, with footballers like Steve Bloomer, kings of their art. Team work replaced individualism, massive concrete terracing enticed thousands of working men in cloth caps. As stadiums grew larger, accidents happened. In 1902, a collapse of terracing during the Scotland-England match at Ibrox Park killed 25 people, the first of the major football disasters in Britain; in 1946, 33 spectators were killed during a FA Cup-tie between Bolton and Stoke at Burnden Park; and in January 1971, 66 fans lost their lives in Britain's worst crowd disaster after a match between Rangers and Celtic.

In the early 1900s footballers earned a maximum of £4 per week, and the first

£1,000 transfer in 1905 caused horror at the FA, who shortly tried to impose a maximum transfer fee of £350.

The 1920s were marked by three memorable events – the first Wembley Cup Final took place in 1923, when a crowd of nearly 150,000 invaded the ground for the match, in which West Ham were beaten by Bolton Wanderers. The second was the change in the offside law, which required two instead of three defenders between attacker and goal. Arsenal were to take advantage of this by using the 'bolt' centre half – the WM formation was born.

proved to be a necessary lesson – and put paid to the baggy shorts era for good. Since the Second World War, the British Isles have thrived on superb footballers – among them, Sir Stanley Matthews, Tom Finney, Billy Wright, John Charles, Wilf Mannion, George Best, Denis Law, Danny Blanchflower, John White, Bobby Charlton, Jim Baxter, Jimmy Greaves, Duncan Edwards, Trevor Francis, Kenny Dalglish, Frank Swift and Gordon Banks – but the international teams have often suffered through a lack of co-operation by clubs in lending

The third was the launching of the World Cup competition in 1928 at a FIFA congress presided over by a Frenchman, Jules Rimet. The first finals took place in Uruguay in 1931, and was won by the host nation. Brazil won the trophy three times after the Second World War and in 1970 were allowed to keep the trophy. England decided not to join this intriguing event until 1950 when they travelled to Brazil and failed dismally, losing 1-0 to the United States in a qualifying match – one of the biggest shocks in football.

Perhaps the most important match England ever lost was a friendly in 1953 against the great Hungarian side by 6-3 – their first defeat by a foreign side at Wembley. It

players. Euphoria greeted England's World Cup win at Wembley under Sir Alf Ramsey's guidance in 1966. But England failed in Mexico in 1970, and failed to qualify for the 1974 and 1978 finals. Scotland put up a poor performance in Argentina in 1978.

While Britain produced exciting postwar club sides like the four European Cup winners, Celtic, Manchester United, Liverpool and Nottingham Forest, the national teams often failed to deliver the goods. And foreign talent flourished with names like di Stefano, Pelé, Puskas, Garrincha, Maradona, Cruyff, Beckenbauer, Gerson and Platini – to them, the game of soccer as a spectacle can be eternally grateful.

This book illustration, captioned 'the association game', is actually of Bayliss of West Bromwich heading towards the Villa goal in the 1887 Cup final, although the colours of the shirts are wrong.

Famous Clubs
Maurice Golesworthy

For many men fame can be fleeting – gone never to return. For others it is elusive and continually comes and goes. A few retain their fame forever. All of this applies equally to football clubs. There were clubs famous a century ago who are now forgotten and even non-existent. The Wanderers are in that category, for they won the FA Cup five times in the first seven years of the competition but disbanded in 1881.

In more modern times Yeovil Town were famous when they knocked First Division Sunderland out of the FA Cup in 1948-49, but that fame was fleeting. Huddersfield Town were famous when they won the League Championship three times in a row in the 1920s, but considering they have not won a major competition for over 50 years would you now rank them among the most famous in the game?

With the spread of the media, especially television, plus the increase in international competitions, one should now judge football fame by world standards rather than by merely domestic ones.

However, before the spread of the media, the first two clubs to become famous, and still retain some of that renown today, were Blackburn Rovers and Preston North End. Neither satisfy our yardstick of worldwide fame, yet they must be included here if only because they established the kind of principles and traditions which help make clubs famous.

There are important similarities between these two Lancashire clubs, for they were both founded by the 'old boy' fraternity and, therefore, formed a link with the earlier amateur clubs. The important distinction is that they were among the first to recognise the need to employ professionals. In this they were democratic. Most old boys' clubs considered football nothing more than a healthy pastime for middle-class Victorian Christian society – many of the earliest clubs were linked with churches or church schools.

Swept up in industrialisation, the northern clubs not only invited the working classes to enjoy a game with them but soon realised that to gain success they needed to 'buy' the most skilful footballers they could find.

It is significant that among the dozen or so most successful English clubs all but two were employing professionals before 1890. Remember that professionalism was not sanctioned by the FA until 1885, yet both Blackburn Rovers and Preston paid footballers before that year, and the part Preston played in forcing the authorities to accept professionalism earned them undying fame.

Preston's leading light, Major William Sudell, took the bull by the horns in 1884 when his club had to answer a charge of professionalism after fielding as many as six Scotsmen in an FA Cup tie. Instead of ducking the issue Sudell frankly admitted paying players and his bold statement certainly precipitated the acceptance of professional footballers.

Blackburn Rovers first shook the amateur football world by reaching the FA Cup Final in 1882. They were beaten 1-0 by the Old Etonians, and the honour of breaking the true blue amateurs' hold on this competition fell to neighbouring Blackburn Olympic, when they beat the Scottish amateur club, Queen's Park, 12 months later.

The amateurs made their last appearances in the Cup final in 1885 and 1886. On both occasions they were represented by Queen's Park and each time they were beaten by Blackburn Rovers. Rovers made it three wins in a row in 1887 when they emerged victorious over West Bromwich Albion.

Nobody has since emulated the Rovers by winning this trophy three seasons in succession, nor indeed has anyone come near their record of 23 consecutive FA Cup ties without defeat.

Two factors have already become apparent which are vital in any assessment of England's most famous clubs – professionalism and the Scottish involvement. Most of the clubs who found fame early on did so because they appreciated the value of introducing Scotsmen who had developed a more successful game of skilful dribbling allied to passing as opposed to the selfish English style of solo runs.

the first of only four English clubs to achieve the 'double'.

Preston's team that season usually included six Scots, or seven if you count John Goodall, who though born in London was brought up in Scotland.

We have already mentioned the next club to earn lasting fame – Aston Villa, and it is a joy to see this great club re-establishing itself among the leaders in the 1980s.

Aston Villa has been one of England's greatest clubs over the years. The most successful of all their sides is this collection of stalwarts – the 1896-97 double-winning side.

In March 1881 Blackburn included four Scotsmen in a team that went to Preston to show North End how the game was played by thrashing them 16-0. Within two or three years Preston were paying a number of Scotsmen, among them Nick Ross, soon to be hailed as "the finest back in the world".

The formation of the Football League in 1888 was a natural adjunct to professionalism, for once clubs had begun paying players they needed more regular fixtures and increased competition to maintain interest and keep the money flowing. The League was the brainchild of another Scot – William McGregor of Aston Villa.

In the first season of this new competition Preston North End earned themselves the title of 'The Invincibles' by winning the Championship without losing a match and also annexing the FA Cup without conceding a goal. So they became

Formed in 1874 they were soon influenced by Scottish dribblers, notably George Ramsay and Archie Hunter, who joined them in 1876 and 1878 respectively. Ramsay served them in various capacities for 59 years until his death in 1935.

Villa is without doubt one of Britain's most successful clubs, having won the FA Cup seven times, the League Championship seven times and the League Cup on three occasions.

They first won the FA Cup in 1887, and from then until the turn of the century were either FA Cup finalists or finished in one of the top two places in the League in nine out of 13 seasons! Indeed, they enjoyed a run of five League Championships and two Cup wins in a spell of only seven seasons from 1893 to 1900. Their greatest campaign was 1896-97 when they became the second club to complete the 'double'.

During this period three other clubs

came into the reckoning among the famous – Wolverhampton Wanderers, Everton and Sunderland, with the last making the greatest impact at that particular time.

Founded by school teachers in 1879 (inspired by a Scotsman) Sunderland's rise to fame was due to an Englishman, Tom Watson from Newcastle, the game's first great professional manager, who appreciated the amount of talent there was North of the Border and annoyed so many Scottish clubs with his numerous 'raids' into their territory. His team that won the Championship in 1891-92 included only one Englishman, and even he joined them from a Scottish club! Watson was in charge of Sunderland from 1889 to 1896 when he took over at Liverpool, and during that period his side became known as the 'Team of All the Talents'.

After losing to Wolves in September 1891 Sunderland did not lose another home League game for over three years. Then our old friends Blackburn Rovers lowered their colours. However, that was followed by another 37 home games without defeat before losing to Bury in September 1896. That was a run of 82 home League games with only one defeat, and during this spell they won the Championship three times in four seasons. In the odd season out they were runners-up to Aston Villa.

Among their Scottish stars was Johnny Campbell, the most prolific goal-scorer of his day and the first to score over 30 goals in a season of First Division matches. In his three Championship seasons he netted 83 in 81 games.

The first part of the twentieth century up to the First World War belonged to Sunderland's neighbours, Newcastle United. A fine close-passing attacking combination, their first major honour came in 1904-05 when they not only won the League Championship but also reached the Cup final to be beaten by Aston Villa. Among their 12 leading players that season Newcastle included seven Scots, the finest of whom was left-half Peter McWilliam, known as 'Peter the Great'.

In a run of seven seasons, 1904-11, United won the League three times and reached the Cup final five times. Unfortunately, Crystal Palace, the Cup final ground of that period at Sydenham, proved something of a hoodoo, for all five of United's attempts to capture the trophy

there failed. Their solitary victory in this spell came in a replay at Goodison Park when they beat Barnsley 2-0 after a 1-1 draw at Crystal Palace. Goalkeeper Jim Lawrence (from Glasgow), winger John Rutherford (a local lad), and the burly centre forward Bill Appleyard (from Cleethorpes) played in all five finals.

A more recent spell of success by this famous club was that in the 1950s when they won the FA Cup three times in five years, thanks largely to local discoveries Bobby Cowell and Jackie Milburn, and Scotsman Bobby 'Dazzler' Mitchell, who played in all three finals.

So far we have mentioned five clubs as having established their fame – Blackburn Rovers, Preston, Aston Villa, Sunderland and Newcastle, with Everton and Wolves also making their mark – all of them from the stronghold of professionalism in the midlands and north. The next of our dozen most famous English clubs to achieve renown is the first from the south – Arsenal.

It is now that we begin to regard fame as being worldwide, for by the time that the Gunners had won their first major honour in 1930 the game had really taken a hold around the globe and the foreigners were beginning to show their prowess. England was first defeated abroad by Spain in 1929, while Scotland's first continental defeat came in Austria in 1931. The first World Cup tournament was held in 1930.

There is little doubt that of all the British clubs Arsenal was first to become world famous. Long before they had won the Championship five times and the FA Cup twice in the 1930s it was often said that even the boys in the jungles of darkest Africa were Arsenal fans. A great deal of this was due to their publicity minded manager, Herbert Chapman. For example, did he not persuade London Transport to name a station after his club!

When we recall that Arsenal did not turn professional until 1891 and remember how they were immediately banned from local competitions and expelled by the London FA, we have an indication as to why the southern clubs had dragged so far behind the leaders in the Midlands and north. Professionalism might well have ended Arsenal's career because of their geographical location, but salvation came through admission to the Second Division of the Football League in 1893 – the first club south of Birmingham to be so elected.

Perhaps the first side to be world famous. The great team of the 1930s was Arsenal. This eleven from 1933-34 is back Sidey, Dunne, Moss, Male, John. Front Hill, Bowden, Jones, James, Bastin, Hapgood.

In the 14 years from when Herbert Chapman joined them in 1925 until the outbreak of the Second World War there were only two seasons in which the Highbury club did not either finish higher than fourth in the First Division or reach the last four in the FA Cup. Often they did both. Their major successes included four Championship titles in five years (five in eight years) and two FA Cup wins. Five Gunners played in all five of those Championship-winning campaigns and must, therefore, rank among the all-time greats: Cliff Bastin, Eddie Hapgood, Joe Hulme, George Male and Herbie Roberts, all Englishmen. To those illustrious names we should add two who played in the first four Championship wins, Scotsman Alex James and Welshman Bob John. Alas, the maestro, Herbert Chapman, did not complete the course, for he died suddenly in 1934.

Arsenal have maintained that aura, for apart from the fact that they currently have the longest uninterrupted run of First Division membership – unbroken since 1919 – they did, of course, become the fourth club to clinch the 'double' in 1970-71.

No club has more First Division experience than Everton who first made their mark as runners-up to Preston in the League's inaugural season and won the Championship the following year. They have now completed 78 seasons in the First Division while Aston Villa (71) and Liverpool (66) are runners-up in this respect. The difficulty with Everton is pinpointing an outstanding period in their history for it is to their credit that their list of successes has been more widespread than most. Since the League was formed in 1888 there have only been two decades in which this club has failed to finish either first or second in the League. Those are the 1940s (largely lost in the war) and the 1950s when they slid into the Second Division for a brief spell.

For sheer excitement we cannot overlook the years between the two World Wars, throughout the greatest part of which Everton were led by that goalscoring genius, Billy 'Dixie' Dean, and won the Championship three times and the FA Cup once. Critics could argue that Everton lacked consistency during this period, and it has to be admitted that their topsy-turvy form defied logical explanation. Yet it was their spectacular recoveries after those breaks in the doldrums that made them such an attraction. One wonders what Everton would have accomplished but for the outbreak of the Second World War, for their team that won the Championship in 1938-39, led so spectacularly by Dean's successor, Tommy Lawton, must be ranked among the club's best.

Since the Second World War Everton have finished as many seasons in the lower half of the First Division as in the top half, but have maintained their position among the more famous by adding two more League Championship wins and an FA Cup victory.

Another club whose call to greatness was delayed by the Second World War was the Wolves. Of course, they had long been well respected, and one of their earliest successes merits a mention here because it was achieved with a team of 11 Englishmen. That was winning the Cup in 1893 by beating favourites Everton. However, it was not until the late 1930s that they proved their prowess in the League by finishing runners-up in both 1937-38 and 1938-39. In that last season they were also surprisingly beaten by Portsmouth in the Cup final.

After the war, however, the Wolves really gained worldwide fame and probably did more than any other club in the 1950s to restore faith in British football which was then at a low ebb. Beaten by the U.S.A. in the 1950 World Cup and thrashed twice by Hungary in 1953 and 1954, English complacency regarding soccer superiority had been badly shaken. Wolves restored British pride by beating Moscow Spartak 4-0, Honved (including Puskas) 3-2, Moscow Dynamo 2-1, Real Madrid (including di Stefano) 3-2, and Borrussia Dortmund 4-3. Wolves' enterprise in arranging these floodlit friendlies, especially the first two mentioned, added a spur to the movement for a European Cup

Moscow Dynamo, the first Russian side to visit Britain, take the field for their first match, against Chelsea at Stamford Bridge. The flowers were presented to the Chelsea team.

The famous Manchester United side known as the 'Busby Babes'. This was the 1957 FA Cup final, a few months before the Munich air disaster which destroyed the team. The players, led by Matt Busby, are Byrne, Berry, Blanchflower, Wood, Foulkes, Charlton, Taylor, Colman, Edwards and Pegg.

competition. It is, therefore, ironic that this famous club has never since been among the winners of any of the European competitions.

Wolves, nevertheless, developed into one of the most prolific goalscoring sides in modern times when they won the Championship twice and the FA Cup in successive seasons 1957-58, 1958-59, 1959-60. Indeed, in the last of those seasons they almost joined the elite of League and Cup 'double' winners, but although heading the table when they completed their programme they were pipped by one point by Burnley, who had a game in hand and won it. After that Wolves' Cup final victory over those old Cup fighters, Blackburn Rovers, was rather an anti-climax. Players who appeared in each of the two Championship-winning campaigns as well as the Cup final were goalkeeper Malcolm Finlayson, full-backs George Showell and Gerry Harris, half-backs Eddie Clamp, Bill Slater and Ron Flowers, and forwards Norman Deeley, Jimmy Murray and Peter Broadbent.

The 1960s were halcyon years for the Manchester clubs, City and United. City won the Championship one season, FA Cup the next and League Cup a year later, but in the matter of honours United must take pride of place, not only because of their domestic successes but because they became the first English club to win the European Cup when they beat Benfica 4-1 after extra time at Wembley in 1968.

United's story is all the more remarkable because their quiet genius, Scotsman Matt Busby, built a team to win the Championship three times in six seasons in the 1950s only to have it almost wiped out in the Munich air crash, then, five years later, came back to win two League Championships and the European Cup, as well as finishing runners-up, all in the space of six seasons! If it's worldwide fame you are seeking then Manchester United has set the pattern, as confirmed by the fan mail they receive from all parts of the globe.

Tottenham Hotspur were another club to earn undying fame in the 1960s for not only were they the first British club to win a major European competition, the Cup-winners' Cup with a smashing 5-1 victory over Atletico Madrid in 1963, but they also became the third to achieve the 'double' in 1960-61 with a wonderfully smooth brand of football inspired and paced by a superb skipper, Danny Blanchflower, the first Irishman we have mentioned in this particular review. Scotsmen also played a part – goalkeeper Bill Brown, powerhouse wing half Dave Mackay, the elusive and ill-fated John White at inside right. England centre forward Bobby Smith, a real block-buster, got the lion's share of the goals.

There is no doubt about the club that perpetuated their fame in the 1970s and right through to the present time, for Liverpool have practically monopolised the major honours during this period, never finishing below second place in a run of eight seasons in which they carried off the Championship five times. During the same spell they also won the FA Cup once, were runners-up once, won the UEFA Cup twice and the European Cup twice, as well as the Super Cup once. No British club has

clubs as being the most famous will surely start arguments about those left out, despite the fact that those named have won over half the total of domestic honours available to over 100 major clubs since 1872. In Scotland, however, there is no doubt about the two top clubs, for Rangers and Celtic have dominated the League and Cup to such an extent that in the 84 seasons since the League began there have only been five in which neither club has won either the League or Cup. Indeed, even in those five seasons one of these two clubs was Championship runners-up!

Leeds United were England's best club for a spell in the late 1960s and early 1970s. Bayern Munich were West Germany's best side at around the same time. This is Leeds, represented by Allan Clarke, kicking, and Bayern, in the person of Franz Beckenbauer, failing to get in a tackle, in the 1975 European Cup Final.

ever enjoyed such a run of international success.

Among the English clubs featured here Liverpool are the youngest, having been formed in 1892 by the owner of the Anfield Ground after the original tenants, Everton, had moved to another ground at Goodison. Among English clubs only Aston Villa have won more domestic competitions than Liverpool, but the Reds come out top when European triumphs are included.

Liverpool's galaxy of stars is blinding but we should mention goalkeeper Ray Clemence, from Skegness, who appeared in all five of their Cup final successes in Europe, plus Emlyn Hughes, from Barrow-in-Furness, and Steve Heighway, from Dublin, who figured in the first four.

My mentioning only a dozen English

There are those who would wish to remind us that the depth of talent in the Scottish League is not what it is in the Football League, but you cannot blame these two Glasgow clubs for that, and such supremacy as they have maintained over such a long period must be worthy of all praise. Remember that, with the majority of Scottish clubs, these two suffered badly through the emigration of their best players to England. The trek began even before the legalisation of professionalism in 1885 and then rose to a flood. It was aggravated by the fact that the Scottish FA refused to accept professionalism until 1893, despite it being general knowledge that many clubs were already paying their players.

The rivalry between Rangers and Celtic is legend. Rangers are older than any other club mentioned in this review (apart from the Wanderers), being formed in 1873 by a bunch of rowing enthusiasts. Celtic were comparatively late on the scene, being formed by Irish Catholics to help collect money to provide food for needy children, but they were the first to make their mark in both League and Cup, enjoying their initial Cup win in 1892 and Championship in 1892-93. No major club anywhere has emulated Celtic's remarkable run of nine successive League Championships in the 1960s and 1970s, although, overall, Rangers still hold the lead in the number of times

history to average over a goal a game throughout his career, while their great centre half, Billy McNeill, is the only player this century to collect seven Scottish Cup winners' medals with a single club. However, no Scottish club has had a player capped as many times as Rangers' favourite, George Young, with a total of 53 appearances 1946-57. In addition Rangers have had more players capped than any other club in Britain, the total being well over the 100 mark.

If we are looking for a straight comparison between these Scottish clubs and the

the Championship has come their way. Celtic take the major share of the honours in the Cup and it would be asking for trouble to try and decide which of these is the more famous. Celtic, of course, were the first British club to win the European Cup when they beat Internazionale 2-1 in 1967. They also reached the final three years later when Feyenoord beat them 2-1 after extra time. Rangers, on the other hand, have reached the final of the European Cup Winners Cup three times, winning it once, in 1972 with a fine 3-2 victory over Moscow Dynamo.

As for the star players these two Scottish giants have produced it would need a whole book to list them, but we can never forget that in Jimmy McGrory Celtic had the only top scorer in British football

top English clubs in major competition we can only look at the various European cups and note that Rangers have beaten Wolves but lost to Spurs, Leeds United and Newcastle United, while Celtic have lost to both Leeds and Liverpool.

Having agreed that true football fame is now worldwide we must acknowledge that there are many renowned clubs beyond our shores and only space precludes us from mentioning a large number. Few fans, however, would argue with the choice of Real Madrid as the most famous. Any club that can win such a pre-eminent competition as the European Champion Clubs Cup seven times, including five times in a row, must rank among the greatest. That footballing genius, Alfredo di Stefano, who led them to all of their first five victories as

Liverpool dominated English soccer throughout the 1970s, and finally won the European Cup in 1977. This is Case taking a free kick as Borussia Moenchengladbach make a wall during the final.

well as in two other finals when they were beaten, scored a record total of 49 goals in this competition. Their brilliant winger, Francisco Gento, made a record 88 appearances including eight finals.

Where Real Madrid taught most clubs a lesson is in raising money for their super stadium, the inspiration of their late President, Don Santiago Bernabeu. When he could not get the funds for his ambitious scheme from the banks he issued bonds to the fans and sold over £200,000 worth in the first few hours. The club has over 60,000 members, each with a vote at the A.G.M.

With two World Championships in the bag West Germany has long been recognised as a leading soccer nation and one of their most famous clubs in recent years has been Bayern Munich. Although formed in 1900 and first winning the League in 1932 they were comparatively unknown outside their small circle of fans before the 1960s, but their rapid rise to fame after first winning the League and Cup 'double' in 1969 has been quite remarkable.

When West Germany won the European Championship in 1972 the team included six players from this Bavarian club. The same number helped West Germany beat England 3-1 at Wembley in April 1972, while this country's squad of 22 players that won the World Cup in 1974 included no less than seven from Bayern Munich. Everyone has sung the praises of the stylish Franz Beckenbauer, while Gerd 'Bomber' Muller was one of the finest goalscorers in European football history – 68 goals in 62 internationals and 37 in the European Cup, which Bayern Munich has won three times in a row. Unfortunately, for the purposes of our comparison, they only met one British club in those three seasons, beating Leeds United 2-0 in the 1975 final. They also beat Leeds in the Fairs Cup in 1971, but the results of their other clashes with British clubs in various European Cup competitions only confuse the issue if we wanted to place our football hierarchy in some sort of order, for while they have eliminated Coventry City, Liverpool and Rangers at one time or another, they have also lost to Liverpool and Rangers. In any event comparisons are odious and can only lead to further argument. Let us be proud that the Football League has more truly famous clubs than any other competition in the world.

52 of the World's Most Famous Clubs

AJAX AMSTERDAM: Formed 1900. Major honours: Dutch League champions: 1917-18, 1918-19, 1930-31, 1931-32, 1933-34, 1936-37, 1938-39, 1946-47, 1956-57, 1959-60, 1965-66, 1966-67, 1967-68, 1969-70, 1971-72, 1972-73, 1976-77, 1978-79, 1979-80. Dutch Cup winners: 1917, 1943, 1961, 1967, 1970, 1971, 1972, 1979. European Cup winners: 1971, 1972, 1973; runners-up 1969. World Club Champions: 1972. Super Cup winners: 1972, 1973.

RSC ANDERLECHT: Formed 1908. Major honours: Belgian League Champions: 1946-47, 1948-49, 1949-50, 1950-51, 1953-54, 1954-55, 1955-56, 1958-59, 1961-62, 1963-64, 1964-65, 1965-66, 1966-67, 1967-68, 1971-72, 1973-74. Belgian Cup winners: 1965, 1972, 1973, 1975, 1976. Fairs Cup: runners-up 1970. European Cup Winners Cup: winners 1976, 1978; runners-up 1977. Super Cup winners: 1978.

ARSENAL: Formed 1886 as Royal Arsenal; Woolwich Arsenal 1891; Arsenal 1913. Major honours: Football League Champions: 1930-31, 1932-33, 1933-34, 1934-35, 1937-38, 1947-48, 1952-53, 1970-71. FA Cup winners: 1930, 1936, 1950, 1971, 1979. Fairs Cup winners: 1970. European Cup Winners Cup: runners-up 1980.

ASTON VILLA: Formed 1874. Major honours: Football League Champions: 1893-94, 1895-96, 1896-97, 1898-99, 1899-1900, 1909-10, 1980-81. FA Cup winners: 1887, 1895, 1897, 1905, 1913, 1920, 1957. Football League Cup winners: 1961, 1975, 1977.

ATLETICO BILBAO: Formed 1898. Major honours: Spanish League Champions: 1929-30, 1930-31, 1933-34, 1935-36, 1942-43, 1955-56. Spanish Cup winners: 1903, 1904, 1910, 1911, 1914, 1915, 1916, 1921, 1923, 1930, 1931, 1932, 1933, 1943, 1944, 1945, 1950, 1955, 1956, 1958, 1969, 1973. UEFA Cup: runners-up 1977.

ATLETICO MADRID: Formed 1923; became Atletico Avacione (Air Force Athletic) after Spanish Civil War until end of Second World War. Major honours: Spanish League Champions: 1939-40, 1940-41, 1949-50, 1950-51, 1965-66, 1969-70, 1972-73, 1976-77. Spanish Cup winners: 1960, 1961, 1965, 1972, 1976. European Cup: runners-up 1974. World Club Champions:
1975. European Cup Winners Cup: winners 1962; runners-up 1963.

AUSTRIA/WAC: Formed 1894 as Vienna Cricket and Football Club; Wiener Amateure Sportverein 1911; Fussball Klub Austria 1925; Austria/WAC 1973. Major honours: Austrian League Champions: 1923-24, 1925-26, 1948-49, 1949-50, 1952-53, 1960-61, 1961-62, 1962-63, 1968-69, 1969-70, 1975-76, 1977-78, 1978-79, 1979-80. Austrian Cup winners: 1948, 1949, 1960, 1962, 1963, 1967, 1971, 1974, 1977, 1980. European Cup Winners Cup: runners-up 1978.

CF BARCELONA: Formed 1899. Major honours: Spanish League Champions: 1928-29, 1944-45, 1947-48, 1948-49, 1951-52, 1952-53, 1958-59, 1959-60, 1973-74. Spanish Cup winners: 1912, 1913, 1920, 1922, 1925, 1926, 1928, 1942, 1951, 1952, 1953, 1957, 1959, 1963, 1968, 1971, 1978. European Cup: runners-up 1961. European Cup Winners Cup winners: 1979; runners-up 1969. European Fairs Cup winners: 1958, 1960, 1966; runners-up 1962.

BAYERN MUNICH: Formed 1900. Major honours: German League Champions: 1931-32. West German League Champions: 1968-69, 1971-72, 1972-73, 1973-74, 1979-80. West German Cup winners: 1957, 1966, 1967, 1969, 1971. World Club Champions: 1976. European Cup winners: 1974, 1975, 1976. European Cup Winners Cup winners: 1967.

The European Cup final of 1974, the first of Bayern Munich's hat-trick. Uli Hoeness scores against Atletico Madrid, one of Spain's stronger sides.

The Merseyside derby is always something special. Everton and Liverpool are among England's most consistently successful clubs. Jimmy Case of Liverpool and Dave Jones of Everton in 1976.

BENFICA: Formed 1904; Sports Lisboa e Benfica, 1907. Major honours: Portuguese League Champions: 1935-36, 1936-37, 1937-38, 1941-42, 1942-43, 1944-45, 1949-50, 1954-55, 1956-57, 1959-60, 1960-61, 1962-63, 1963-64, 1964-65, 1966-67, 1967-68, 1968-69, 1970-71, 1971-72, 1972-73, 1974-75, 1975-76, 1976-77. Portuguese Cup winners: 1929, 1930, 1935, 1940, 1943, 1944, 1949, 1951, 1952, 1953, 1955, 1957, 1959, 1962, 1964, 1969, 1970, 1972, 1980. European Cup winners: 1961, 1962; runners-up 1963, 1965, 1968.

BLACKBURN ROVERS: Formed 1875. Major honours: Football League Champions: 1911-12, 1913-14. FA Cup winners: 1884, 1885, 1886, 1890, 1891, 1928.
BOLTON WANDERERS: Formed 1874 as Christ Church FC; Bolton Wanderers 1877. Major honours: FA Cup winners: 1923, 1926, 1929, 1958.
BORRUSSIA MOENCHENGLADBACH: Formed 1900. Major honours: West German League Champions: 1969-70, 1970-71, 1974-75, 1975-76, 1976-77. West German Cup winners: 1960, 1973.

The 1980 European Cup winners, and the 1980 South American Club Cup winners meet for the World Club Championship. Esparrago, captain of Nacional, the winners, in a race for the ball with Ian Wallace of Nottingham Forest.

European Cup: runners-up 1977. UEFA Cup winners: 1975, 1979; runners-up 1973, 1980.

CELTIC: Formed 1887. Major honours: Scottish League Champions: 1892-93, 1893-94, 1895-96, 1897-98, 1904-05, 1905-06, 1906-07, 1907-08, 1909-10, 1913-14, 1914-15, 1915-16, 1916-17, 1918-19, 1921-22, 1925-26, 1935-36, 1937-38, 1953-54, 1965-66, 1966-67, 1967-68, 1968-69, 1969-70, 1970-71, 1971-72, 1972-73, 1973-74, 1980-81. Scottish Cup winners: 1892, 1899, 1900, 1904, 1907, 1908, 1911, 1912, 1914, 1923, 1925, 1927, 1931, 1933, 1937, 1951, 1954, 1965, 1967, 1969, 1971, 1972, 1974, 1975, 1977, 1980. Scottish League Cup winners: 1956-57, 1957-58, 1965-66, 1966-67, 1967-68, 1968-69, 1969-70, 1974-75. European Cup winners: 1967; runners-up 1970.

DUKLA PRAGUE: Formed 1947 as ATK Prague as Czech army club; re-named UDA (Ustedni Dum Armady – Central Club of the Army) 1953; became Dukla 1956. Major honours: Czech League Champions: 1953, 1956, 1957-58,

The Manchester derby. There is not much between the records of the two Manchester clubs over the years. Here United's centre forward Joe Jordan shields the ball from City's Tommy Caton.

27

1960-61, 1961-62, 1962-63, 1963-64, 1965-66, 1976-77, 1978-79. Czech Cup winners: 1961, 1965, 1966, 1969.

EINTRACHT FRANKFURT: Formed 1899 as Frankurter Sportgemeinde Eintracht. Major honours: West German League Champions: 1958-59. West German Cup winners: 1974, 1975. European Cup: runners-up 1960. UEFA Cup winners: 1980.

EVERTON: Formed 1878 as St. Domingo Church Sunday School FC; became Everton 1879. Major honours: Football League Champions: 1890-91, 1914-15, 1927-28, 1931-32, 1938-39, 1962-63, 1969-70. FA Cup winners: 1906, 1933, 1966.

FERENCVAROS: Formed 1899 as FTC Ferencvaros 1927; Kinizsi 1945; temporarily absorbed by Honved until revived as Ferencvaros. Major honours: Hungarian League Champions: 1903, 1905, 1906-07, 1909, 1910, 1911, 1912, 1913, 1926, 1927, 1928, 1932, 1934, 1938, 1940, 1941, 1949, 1964, 1967, 1968, 1976. Hungarian Cup winners: 1913, 1922, 1933, 1935, 1942, 1943, 1944, 1958, 1972, 1974, 1976, 1978. European Cup Winners Cup: runners-up 1975. European Fairs Cup winners: 1965; runners-up 1968.

SC FEYENOORD: Formed 1908. Major honours: Dutch League Champions: 1923-24, 1927-28, 1935-36, 1937-38, 1939-40, 1960-61, 1961-62, 1964-65, 1968-69, 1970-71, 1973-74. Dutch Cup winners: 1930, 1935, 1965, 1969, 1980. World Club Champions: 1970. European Cup winners: 1970. UEFA Cup winners: 1974.

HEART OF MIDLOTHIAN: Formed 1873. Major honours: Scottish League Champions: 1894-95, 1896-97, 1957-58, 1959-60, 1979-80. Scottish Cup winners: 1891, 1896, 1901, 1906, 1956. Scottish League Cup winners: 1954-55, 1958-59, 1959-60, 1962-63.

HIBERNIAN: Formed 1875 as Edinburgh Hibernians. Major honours: Scottish League Champions: 1902-03, 1947-48, 1950-51, 1951-52. Scottish Cup winners: 1887, 1902. Scottish League Cup winners: 1972-73, 1973-74.

HONVED: Formed 1949 absorbing the Budapest club, Kispest. Hungarian League Champions: 1949-50 (Autumn), 1950 (Spring), 1952, 1954, 1955. Hungarian Cup winners: 1926 (as Kispest), 1964.

INTERNAZIONALE (INTER-MILAN): Formed 1909 by breakaway group from AC Milan; merged with US Milanese 1928 as Ambrosiana Internazionale; became Internazionale again in 1945. Major honours: Italian League Champions: 1909-10, 1919-20, 1929-30, 1937-38, 1939-40, 1952-53, 1953-54, 1962-63, 1964-65, 1965-66, 1970-71, 1979-80. Italian Cup winners: 1978. World Club Champions: 1964, 1965. European Cup winners: 1964, 1965; runners-up 1967, 1972.

JUVENTUS: Formed 1897 as Sport Club Juventus; became Juventus FC 1899. Major honours: Italian League Champions: 1905, 1925-26, 1930-31, 1931-32, 1932-33, 1933-34, 1934-35, 1949-50, 1951-52, 1957-58, 1959-60, 1960-61, 1966-67, 1971-72, 1974-75, 1976-77, 1977-78. Italian Cup winners: 1959, 1960, 1965, 1979. European Cup: runners-up 1973. European Fairs Cup: runners-up 1965, 1971. UEFA Cup winners: 1977.

LEEDS UNITED: Formed 1919 after older Leeds City club (formed 1904) had been wound up. Major honours: Football League Champions: 1968-69, 1973-74. FA Cup winners: 1971-72. Football League Cup winners: 1968. European Cup: runners-up 1975. European Cup Winners Cup: runners-up 1973. European Fairs Cup winners: 1968, 1971; runners-up 1967.

LIVERPOOL: Formed 1892. Major honours: Football League Champions: 1900-01, 1905-06, 1921-22, 1922-23, 1946-47, 1963-64, 1965-66, 1972-73, 1975-76, 1976-77, 1978-79, 1979-80. FA Cup winners: 1965, 1974. Football League Cup winners: 1981. European Cup winners: 1977, 1978, 1981. European Cup Winners Cup: runners-up 1966. UEFA Cup winners: 1973, 1976. Super Cup winners: 1978.

MANCHESTER CITY: Formed 1894 out of an older club, Ardwick, that had gone out of existence through lack of funds. Ardwick had been formed in 1887 by amalgamation of West Gorton and Gorton Athletic. Major honours: Football League Champions: 1936-37, 1967-68. FA Cup winners: 1904, 1934, 1956, 1969. Football League Cup winners: 1970, 1976. European Cup Winners Cup winners: 1970.

MANCHESTER UNITED: Formed 1902 after predecessor, Newton Heath (1880) had gone bankrupt. Major honours: Football League Champions: 1907-08, 1910-11, 1951-52, 1955-56, 1956-57, 1964-65, 1966-67. FA Cup winners: 1909, 1948, 1963, 1977. European Cup winners: 1968.

AC MILAN: Formed 1899 as Milan Cricket and Football Club; Milan Associazione Sportiva 1930; Milan Associazione Calcio 1939. Major honours: Italian League Champions: 1901, 1906, 1907, 1950-51, 1954-55, 1956-57, 1958-59, 1961-62, 1967-68, 1978-79. Italian Cup winners: 1967, 1972, 1973, 1977. World Club Champions: 1969. European Cup winners: 1963, 1969; runners-up 1958. European Cup Winners Cup winners: 1968, 1973; runners-up 1974.

MOSCOW DYNAMO: Formed as Orekhovo 1887; became OKS (Orekhovo Klub Sport) 1907; later known as Morosovtsi, and became Dynamo when adopted by the Soviet Electrical Trades Union. Major honours: Russian League Champions: 1936 (Spring), 1937, 1940, 1945, 1949, 1954, 1955, 1957, 1959, 1963, 1976 (jointly with Torpedo Moscow). Russian Cup winners: 1937, 1953, 1967, 1970, 1977. European Cup Winners Cup: runners-up 1972.

MOSCOW SPARTAK: Formed 1922. Major honours: Russian League Champions: 1936 (Autumn), 1938, 1939, 1952, 1953, 1956, 1958, 1962, 1969, 1979. Russian Cup winners: 1938, 1939, 1946, 1947, 1950, 1958, 1963, 1965, 1971.

MTK-VM BUDAPEST: Formed 1888 from an old Gymnastic and Athletic Club which had been founded by British students. Has since gone under several different names: Hungaria, Textilesek, Bastya, Vörös Lobogo (Red Banner) and MTK since 1956. Major honours: Hungarian League Champions: 1904, 1908, 1914, 1917, 1918, 1919, 1920, 1921, 1922, 1923, 1925, 1929, 1953, 1958. Hungarian Cup winners: 1968. European Cup Winners Cup: runners-up 1964.

NACIONAL: Formed 1899 by amalgamation of Montevideo and Defensor. Major honours: Uruguayan League Champions: 1902, 1903, 1912, 1915, 1916, 1917, 1919, 1920, 1922, 1923, 1924, 1933, 1934, 1939, 1940, 1941, 1942, 1943, 1946, 1947, 1950, 1952, 1955, 1956, 1957, 1963, 1966, 1969, 1970, 1971, 1972, 1977, 1980. South American Club Cup winners: 1971, 1980; runners-up 1964, 1967, 1969. World Club Champions: 1971, 1981.

NEWCASTLE UNITED: Formed 1882 as Newcastle East End; became Newcastle United 1892. Major honours: Football League Champions: 1904-05, 1906-07, 1908-09, 1926-27. FA Cup winners: 1910, 1924, 1932, 1951, 1952, 1955. European Fairs Cup winners: 1969.

NOTTINGHAM FOREST: Formed 1865. Major honours: Football League Champions 1977-78. FA Cup winners: 1898, 1959. Football League Cup winners: 1978, 1979; runners-up 1980. European Cup winners: 1979, 1980. Super Cup winners: 1980.

The most successful clubs of Italy and Portugal in recent years are Internazionale and Benfica. They met in the 1963 European Cup final, when Eusebio scored this goal for Benfica.

PENAROL: Formed 1891 as Central Uruguayan Railway Cricket Club; became CA Penarol 1913. Major honours: Uruguayan League Champions: 1900, 1901, 1905, 1907, 1911, 1918, 1921, 1926, 1928, 1929, 1932, 1935, 1936, 1937, 1938, 1944, 1945, 1949, 1951, 1953, 1954, 1958, 1959, 1960, 1961, 1962, 1964, 1965, 1967, 1968, 1973, 1974, 1975, 1978, 1979. South American Cup winners: 1960, 1961, 1966. World Club Champions: 1961, 1966.

PRESTON NORTH END: Formed 1881 by members of the North End Cricket and Rugby Club which had been in existence since 1867 (playing rugby from 1879). Major honours: Football League Champions: 1888-89, 1889-90. FA Cup winners: 1889, 1938.

RANGERS: Formed 1873. Major honours: Scottish League Champions: 1898-99, 1899-1900, 1900-01, 1901-02, 1910-11, 1911-12, 1912-13, 1917-18, 1919-20, 1922-23, 1923-24, 1924-25, 1926-27, 1927-28, 1928-29, 1929-30, 1930-31, 1932-33, 1933-34, 1934-35, 1936-37, 1938-39, 1946-47, 1948-49, 1949-50, 1952-53, 1955-56, 1956-57, 1958-59, 1960-61, 1962-63, 1963-64, 1974-75. Scottish Cup winners: 1894, 1897, 1898, 1903, 1928, 1930, 1932, 1934, 1935, 1948, 1949, 1950, 1953, 1960, 1962, 1963, 1964, 1966, 1973, 1976, 1978, 1979, 1981. Scottish League Cup winners: 1946-47, 1948-49, 1960-61, 1961-62, 1963-64, 1964-65, 1970-71, 1975-76, 1977-78, 1978-79. European Cup Winners Cup winners: 1972; runners-up 1961, 1967.

REAL MADRID: Formed 1898. Title 'Real' (Royal) bestowed by King Alfonso XIII 1920. Major honours: Spanish League Champions: 1931-32, 1932-33, 1953-54, 1954-55, 1956-57, 1957-58, 1960-61, 1961-62, 1962-63, 1963-64, 1964-65, 1966-67, 1967-68, 1968-69, 1971-72, 1974-75, 1975-76, 1977-78, 1978-79, 1979-80. Spanish Cup winners: 1905, 1906, 1907, 1908, 1917, 1934, 1936, 1946, 1947, 1962, 1970, 1974, 1975, 1980. World Club Champions: 1960. European Cup winners: 1956, 1957, 1958, 1959, 1960, 1966; runners-up 1962, 1964, 1981. European Cup Winners Cup: runners-up 1971.

RED STAR BELGRADE: Formed 1945 by Belgrade University students. Major honours: Yugoslavian League Champions: 1950-51, 1952-53, 1955-56, 1956-57, 1958-59, 1959-60, 1963-64, 1967-68, 1968-69, 1969-70, 1972-73, 1976-77, 1979-80. Yugoslavian Cup winners: 1948,

1949, 1950, 1958, 1959, 1964, 1968, 1970, 1971. UEFA Cup: runners-up 1979.

RAPID VIENNA: Formed 1898. Major honours: Austrian League Champions: 1911-12, 1912-13, 1915-16, 1916-17, 1918-19, 1919-20, 1920-21, 1922-23, 1928-29, 1934-35, 1937-38, 1939-40, 1940-41, 1946-47, 1950-51, 1953-54, 1955-56, 1956-57, 1959-60, 1963-64, 1966-67, 1967-68. Austrian Cup winners: 1946, 1961, 1968, 1969, 1972, 1976.

SAINT ETIENNE: Formed 1933. Major honours: French League Champions: 1956-57, 1963-64, 1966-67, 1967-68, 1968-69, 1969-70, 1973-74, 1974-75, 1975-76. French Cup winners: 1962, 1968, 1970, 1974, 1975, 1977. European Cup: runners-up 1976.

SANTOS: Formed 1912. São Paulo League (Brazil) Champions: 1935, 1955, 1956, 1958, 1959, 1960, 1961, 1963, 1965, 1967, 1968, 1969, 1973. Brazilian League Champions: 1968. World Club Champions: 1962, 1963. South American Cup winners: 1962, 1963.

SHEFFIELD UNITED: Formed 1889. Major honours: Football League Champions: 1897-98. FA Cup winners: 1899, 1902, 1915, 1925.

SHEFFIELD WEDNESDAY: Formed 1867. Major honours: Football League Champions: 1902-03, 1903-04, 1928-29, 1929-30. FA Cup winners: 1896, 1907, 1935.

SUNDERLAND: Formed 1879 as Sunderland and District Teachers AFC; adopted present title 1881. Major honours: Football League Champions: 1891-92, 1892-93, 1894-95, 1901-02, 1912-13, 1935-36. FA Cup winners: 1937, 1973.

TORINO: Formed 1906. Major honours: Italian League Champions: 1942-43, 1945-46, 1946-47, 1947-48, 1948-49, 1975-76. Italian Cup winners: 1936, 1943, 1968, 1971.

TOTTENHAM HOTSPUR: Formed 1882. Major honours: Football League Champions: 1950-51, 1960-61. FA Cup winners: 1901, 1921, 1961, 1962, 1967, 1981. Football League Cup winners: 1970-71, 1972-73. European Cup Winners Cup winners: 1963. UEFA Cup winners: 1972; runners-up 1974.

UJPESTI-DOZSA: Formed 1899 as Ujpesti; became Ujpesti-Dozsa in 1957. Major honours: Hungarian League Champions: 1930, 1931, 1933, 1935, 1945, 1947, 1960, 1969, 1970, 1971, 1972, 1973, 1974,

1975. Hungarian Cup winners: 1969, 1970, 1971, 1975. European Fairs Cup: runners-up 1969.

WEST BROMWICH ALBION: Formed 1879. Major honours: Football League Champions: 1919-20. FA Cup winners: 1888, 1892, 1931, 1954, 1968. Football League Cup winners: 1965-66.

WEST HAM UNITED: Formed as Thames Ironworks FC 1895; adopted present title 1900, when a new company was formed. Major honours: FA Cup winners: 1964, 1975, 1980. European Cup Winners Cup winners: 1965; runners-up 1976.

WOLVERHAMPTON WANDERERS: Formed 1877 as St Lukes; adopted present title 1880. Major honours: Football League Champions: 1953-54, 1957-58, 1958-59. FA Cup winners: 1893, 1908, 1949, 1960. Football League Cup winners: 1974, 1980. UEFA Cup: runners-up 1972.

A Gallery of Great Players

Peter Arnold

Osvaldo Ardiles

Ardiles became a favourite with soccer fans throughout the world during the World Cup finals in his native Argentina in 1978. Not only was he easily recognisable with his hawk-like face and slim build, but he seemed to attract the ball as he bustled around in midfield. Not equipped physically to win the ball with robust methods, he specialised in neat interceptions and good positional play, and once in possession he always went forward to make the telling pass. Against Poland he ran almost the length of the pitch to make a goal for Kempes, and in the World Cup final itself it was his coolness when all around were concentrating on the physical battle which provided Kempes with the chance to open the scoring against Holland.

Born on 3 August 1952 in Cordoba, he played alongside his friend Kempes in the Instituto de Cordoba side before joining Huracan BA. On 10 July 1978 Spurs manager Keith Burkinshaw signed Ardiles and fellow-Argentinian Ricardo Villa for a combined fee of about £750,000, and he was an immediate success in English soccer. In the 1979 Football Writers Association Player of the Year awards he finished runner-up to Kenny Dalglish.

An intelligent man, he was soon at home with English interviewers and continued to study law. He played for Argentina in the Gold Cup Tournament for World Cup winning nations in 1981, bringing his total of caps till then to 44. Already with a World Cup winner's medal, he won an FA Cup winner's medal in 1981 with Spurs.

Gordon Banks

Voted the best goalkeeper of the 1966 World Cup tournament, Gordon Banks was generally accepted for a number of years as simply the best goalkeeper in the world, a view endorsed by Pelé after Banks had made a memorable save from him during the World Cup finals of 1970 – a save which television replays have made about the most famous ever.

Banks was born on 30 December 1937 at Sheffield. He made his debut for Chesterfield in 1958, and played one season before Leicester City signed him. He played seven seasons for Leicester, and helped them to two losing FA Cup final appearances while making himself an automatic first choice for England. In 1966 he conceded only three goals while England won the World Cup. Stoke bought him for £52,500 in 1967, and he helped them win their first-ever honour in over 100 years' history – a League Cup success in 1972.

He was still the world's best goalkeeper, and, indeed, the Footballer of the Year, when later in 1972 a car crash deprived him of the sight of one eye. He soldiered on for a while, making himself popular as Fort Lauderdale's goalkeeper in the United States, but eventually gave up. As well as a World Cup winner's medal he won League Cup winner's medals with Leicester and Stoke, and 73 caps, a record for an England goalkeeper.

Franz Beckenbauer

'Elegance' was the most-used epithet to describe the style of Kaiser Franz, the complete footballer. He was the leading player in West Germany's resurgence to soccer power in the 1970s. His honours could lead him to claim he was the world's most successful footballer: after he had played for West Germany in the World Cups of 1966 (runners-up) and 1970 (third) he led them to success in 1974. He also led West Germany to the European Championship in 1972 and the final again in 1976. His club Bayern Munich won the German 'Bundesliga' in 1969, 1972, 1973 and 1974 and he led them to three European Cups in 1974, 1975 and 1976, as well as the World Club Championship in 1976. He was European Footballer of the Year in 1972 and 1976.

Franz Beckenbauer, who after tremendous success in Europe went off to the States to replace Pelé at New York Cosmos.

Beckenbauer then went off to play three seasons for New York Cosmos, but such was his value that when Hamburg signed him for his return to Germany in 1980 he was stated to be that country's highest-paid player.

Born on 11 September 1945, he won 103 caps for West Germany, forfeiting more by going to America. But it was his style of play that was memorable. He invented a central sweeping role that made him at once part of the back four and a midfield prompter of attacks. He also scored important goals, including the one that began West Germany's late rally to beat holders England in the 1970 World Cup quarter-finals, and he did it all without ever seeming to hurry.

George Best

George Best was a footballing genius, whose only handicap was that he had some of the waywardness and rebelliousness that sometimes go with genius but are found to be drawbacks in footballers. A natural winger, his balance, dribbling, speed, shooting and heading made him a match-winner in any company. Could he have played in the World Cup finals with a strong team, he might have rivalled Pelé in the world's estimation, but Northern Ireland were never strong enough, and the tough physical style of the English First Division eventually disillusioned him. He often claimed that British referees were unable to protect him adequately from fouls.

Born on 22 May 1946 in Belfast, he made his first appearance for Manchester United when 17 in 1962 and played for them, despite wrangles, disappearances and suspensions until 1974, when both he and club had had enough. He subsequently played for Stockport, Fulham, Hibs and Los Angeles Aztecs, not without more troubles.

The first footballer to have a pop star image, his off-the-field antics were frequently front page news. But as a footballer he won two Championship medals with United and a European Cup winner's medal (his individual goal against Benfica in the final will be long remembered). In 1968 he was both British and European Footballer of the Year. He played 37 times for Northern Ireland, making his last appearance in 1978, when long past his best. Many who saw the exciting skills of his prime cannot believe there was ever a better player.

Trevor Brooking

There are those (and Brian Clough is among them) who would not pick Trevor Brooking for England, let alone a gallery of great players. They point to his softness in the tackle, lack of a blistering shot, unexceptional heading skill and leisurely pace. Brooking's fans would assert that his ability to play the game at his own speed, his positional sense and constructive awareness are refreshing in an age of high speed erratic soccer. Despite the alleged softness, he is a difficult man to dispossess, he can beat a man with a subtle dip of his shoulders, and he only needs half a yard anyway in which to measure his passes.

Brooking is an old-fashioned footballer in some respects, including his loyalty to West Ham United, for whom he has played, usually in the Second Division, since his debut in 1967. Born in 1948, at Barking, Essex, he made his England debut in 1974, and to the end of the 1979-80 season had won 40 caps as a deep-lying inside forward. He won FA Cup winner's medals in 1975 and 1980, when he scored the only goal at Wembley. Not given to robust play, he remains unruffled after being fouled, and his presence in a match ensures that no matter what mayhem, dash and workrate is going on elsewhere on the pitch some polished football will be provided. And at the end of the day, it will often be found that a cool touch from Brooking has decided the match.

John Charles

The most striking thing about John Charles was his physique. Standing 6 ft 1 in and weighing 13 st 12 lb, he had a magnificent chest, a long neck for powerful headers, and comparatively short thick legs which gave him good control on the ground. A great centre half, his powerful shooting made him just as good a centre forward, and he could reasonably be picked in a best-ever eleven in either position.

Born on Christmas Eve, 1931, in Swansea, he played for Swansea Town as a schoolboy. Leeds United signed him as a professional in 1949, and moved him from centre half to centre forward, where he soon achieved a club record of 42 goals in a season. He made his debut for Wales in 1950, and was often picked at centre half, centre forward or inside forward in the same season.

Trevor Brooking, for whom 1981 meant First Division football once again for West Ham United.

Osvaldo Ardiles of Spurs, about to be tackled by Hunt of Coventry, made the transition from Argentine pitches to the mud of an English winter with his usual unruffled efficiency.

Two of the all-time greats in opposition. Gordon Banks of England clearing the ball with George Best of Northern Ireland in attendance during the home international tournament of 1972.

Kenny Dalglish playing for Scotland against Argentina in the pre-1978 World Cup tour.

In 1957 he went to Juventus in Italy for £65,000 and was an outstanding success, transforming Juventus from a struggling club to three times champions and twice Cup winners. Despite his strength, his temperament was immaculate, and he was called *il buon gigante*, the gentle giant. He returned to Leeds in 1962, but preferring the slower pace and greater sophistication of Italian football returned to play for Roma after only one season. But his best was past, and he came back to Cardiff City after only ten games. He won 38 caps for Wales, and played in the World Cup finals of 1958.

Bobby Charlton

Bobby Charlton was just getting into the brilliant Manchester United side when the Munich air crash of 1958 destroyed the team and took away from him so many of his friends. Charlton survived, and three months later made his debut for England. Public sympathy and his talent for scoring exciting goals made him Britain's best-loved footballer.

Born on 11 October 1937 at Ashington, he enjoyed a long career which brought him every honour in the game. Perhaps his two greatest moments were winning the World Cup in 1966 and, considering the

Munich disaster occurred when United were returning from a successful European Cup-tie, the winning of the European Cup in 1968, the first victory by an English club.

Although such a fine goal-scorer, Charlton's best role was as an attacking mid-field player, where his characteristic shoulder-dipping swerve enabled him to beat opponents at speed and approach goal from deep positions. Charlton in full flight towards goal was a sight which always filled crowds with excitement and expectancy. A one-club man, he made 606 League appearances for United between 1956 and 1973, a club record, as were his 198 goals. He won three Championship medals, a Cup winner's medal and a European Cup winner's medal to add to his World Cup winner's medal. He was Footballer of the Year in 1966, and European Footballer of the Year in 1968. His record of 106 matches for England has since been beaten, but his 49 goals for England remains a record. He made the name 'Bobby Charlton' recognised and respected throughout the world in a remarkable career.

Johan Cruyff

On the retirement of Pelé, Johan Cruyff became the popular choice as the best footballer in the world.

Born on 25 April 1947 about 100 metres from the Ajax stadium in Amsterdam, he showed precocious skills as a boy and joined Ajax when he was 15, winning his first Championship medal when he was 19. His main assets were a lightning-quick brain which enabled him to spot the best moves to make in a match, phenomenal acceleration, and ball control which left opponents floundering. An ability to score goals early in his career became secondary later to his constructive skills which more often made goals for others.

In domestic football for Ajax he won seven Championship medals, three Cup winner's medals, three European Cup winner's medals and a World Club Championship medal. In 1973 he was transferred to Barcelona for the equivalent of a then astonishing world record £922,300, and won a Spanish Championship medal in 1974 and a Cup winner's medal in 1978. He was three times European Footballer of the Year.

He won 52 caps for Holland, and as captain in the 1970s when Holland were the most exciting national team in the world, he suffered the disappointment of losing in the World Cup final of 1974, when West Germany won 2-1.

Towards the end of his playing days Cruyff concentrated on his fabulously rich business career. He played at times for New York Cosmos, Los Angeles Aztecs and Washington Diplomats before returning to advise Ajax in 1981, and then join Spanish Second Division club Levante.

Kenny Dalglish

Liverpool's continuous success in the 1970s, and the consequent numerous appearances on television, have made Kenny Dalglish one of the most exposed of modern footballers. Everybody in Britain knows his style – how he shields the ball with his body around the penalty area, how he twists and turns to get a yard of space and how he then lays the ball off or gets in a well-directed shot. Yet he remains an enigma. A consistent match-winner through the hard slog of a First Division season, he often seems unable to dominate as he should at top international level.

Born on 5 April 1948 in Glasgow, Dalglish made 204 League appearances for Celtic in 10 years before being transferred in 1977 for £440,000 to Liverpool, where he replaced Keegan, who had gone to Germany. He won honours in all the Scottish competitions as an inside forward with Celtic and two Championship medals, a Football League Cup winner's medal and a European Cup winner's medal with Liverpool, scoring the only goal in the 1978 European Cup final against Bruges. At the end of the 1979-80 season he had won 75 caps for Scotland, a record, and he appeared in the World Cup final tournaments of 1974 and 1978.

Alfredo di Stefano

An Argentinian whose main successes came in Europe, Alfredo di Stefano was the first post-war player to lay claim to the title of best footballer in the world. Nominally a centre forward, he was an early exponent of total football, being involved on all parts of the pitch, defending, scoring and as captain generally running the whole game.

Born on 4 July 1926 in Barracas, Argentina, he first played for River Plate, winning an Argentine Championship medal in 1947. He then went to Bogota in Colombia, where a few British players also sought big money in a league outside the jurisdiction

of FIFA. He joined Millonarios, and won three Colombian Championship medals. In 1954 he signed for Real Madrid, where he added seven Spanish Championship medals to his collection. It was success all the way for di Stefano, and when the European Cup was instituted he led the great Real Madrid side to victories in the first five tournaments, scoring in each of the finals, including a hat-trick in the marvellous 7-3 defeat of Eintracht Frankfurt at Glasgow in 1960. He was European Footballer of the Year in 1957 and 1959.

He made seven appearances for Argentina and 31 for Spain, although he missed the 1962 World Cup finals through injury. In 1980 he was still in the news, managing Valencia to their European Cup Winners Cup victory over Arsenal.

Duncan Edwards

The only doubt about Duncan Edwards' place in a gallery of greats concerns whether or not at the time of his tragic death in the Munich air crash he had already achieved greatness or 'merely' promised to be the greatest player that ever lived.

Some idea of the physique of the young Duncan Edwards is conveyed by this practice session photograph.

Born on 1 October 1936 in Dudley, Worcestershire, he was only 21 when he died. Sir Matt Busby said he was already the complete footballer. He joined Manchester United on the earliest possible date, his sixteenth birthday, was a First Division player six months later, and an England Under-23 player soon after his seventeenth birthday. He was the youngest-ever full international at 18 years and 183 days old.

A left-half of tremendous physical power

Eusebio

Born Ferreira da Silva on 5 January 1942 at Lourenço Marques, Mozambique, Eusebio became the first great footballer to come out of Africa. He learned the game with the Sporting Club of Lourenço Marques, and joined Benfica of Lisbon in 1961.

An attacking inside forward, he first made an international mark in Benfica's 5-3 defeat of Real Madrid in the European Cup final of 1962. He scored twice, and

The ball is in Forest colours and Trevor Francis appears to be making sure it's his as he leaves Wolves defenders well beaten.

(he was nearly 6 ft tall and weighed 13 stone at 16) he had a crunching tackle, superb positional sense, accuracy in passing with either foot and a thundering shot. He won two Championship medals with the Busby Babes, and was deprived of a Cup winner's medal and a share of the 'double' when United's keeper was injured in the first minutes of the pre-substitute final of 1957. He played, of course, for England schoolboys and the Under-23s, and won 18 full caps, scoring five goals. All this in such a short career. A perfect sportsman, his life is commemorated in a stained glass window in his church at Dudley, showing him in United strip with the legend 'God is with us for our Captain'.

again in the final the following year. In 1963 he played for the Rest of the World team against England in the FA Centenary match.

Eusebio won no fewer than 11 Portuguese Championship medals and five Cup winner's medals with Benfica, as well as a European Cup winner's medal. He was capped 63 times for Portugal, and perhaps his finest hours were in the 1966 World Cup finals in England, where his cannon-ball shot became famous. He was the tournament's best forward, and his nine goals won him the award for the leading scorer. A superb athlete, with exhilarating ball control and speed, he was European Footballer of the Year in 1965.

Tom Finney

According to Bill Shankly, who played behind him at Preston, Finney was England's greatest footballer. Although best remembered for his dazzling dribbling and speed on the wing, he was a complete attacking footballer, and played for England in four positions in the forward line.

He was born on 5 April 1922 in Preston, and signed for Preston straight from school, but had to wait until after the war for his career to begin in earnest. His impact was immediate, and two of his greatest games came early. He was brilliant in 10-0 and 4-0 England wins in Portugal and Italy in 1947 and 1948.

A slight man, with a reputation for sportsmanship despite the hard knocks his ball control earned, he played his entire career for Preston, playing 565 games and scoring nearly 250 goals, 187 in the League, a record for Preston – and most of them came from the wing. Most of that time Preston were a First Division side, and throughout his stay Finney *was* Preston.

The season after he retired they were relegated, and never returned to the top flight.

He never won a Championship or Cup winner's medal – Preston's defeat in the final of 1954 disappointed his many fans – but played 76 times for England, and his 30 goals was at the time a record. He was Footballer of the Year in 1954 and 1957. Sometimes known as 'The Preston Plumber' while playing, he later built up a flourishing plumbing business in his native town.

Trevor Francis

The career of Trevor Francis started spectacularly, went into decline for a few seasons and then blossomed as he established himself as England's most exciting goal-scoring forward. In the course of a decade he went from a 16-year-old £8 per week apprentice to England's first £1 million footballer.

Born on 19 April 1954 in Plymouth, Francis went from school to Birmingham

Left *Eusebio, the Black Panther from Mozambique, lithe, explosive and loaded with winner's medals.*

Right *Tom Finney, the plumber from Preston, with no medals at all, but undoubtedly one of the world's greatest footballers.*

City, making his debut at Cardiff in 1970. At one point he scored 11 goals in six matches, and finished his first season with 15 in 21 games, including four in one match. He then helped England to win the UEFA Youth Cup and in his second season played well as Birmingham won promotion and reached the FA Cup semi-final. Then things went wrong. Picked for England in 1974 he missed his cap through injury, and illness also caused him to miss many games in his first four seasons in the top flight. Eventually, he played for England in 1977 against Holland.

He remained unable to fulfil his brilliant early promise, but Nottingham Forest bought him on 9 February 1979 for £975,000, which with the levy and VAT cost Forest £1,150,500. He made his debut next day in the third team before a crowd of 40. He still had his troubles – an earlier contract obliged him to spend the summer playing for Detroit, and Brian Clough seemed not altogether satisfied with his play.

Finally he got back to his best, and scored the only goal in Forest's 1-0 European Cup final victory over Malmo in 1979. Then injury struck again, and he missed Forest's second European Cup win in 1980 and the European Championship matches the same year.

Luckily, when he returned he seemed as good as ever, and it is to be hoped that he can now settle down to a period of fitness and add to his 18 caps. On his day he plays with more speed and urgency than any other England player, and his skills are badly needed in the national team.

Jimmy Greaves

The supreme gift of Jimmy Greaves was to score goals. Never has there been a player who remained so cool in the penalty area. Because of his knack of being on the right spot at the right time, many of his goals appeared routine, but this says nothing, of course, of the instinctive anticipation of the true goal-scorer, or of the priceless quality of a forward who, given a routine chance, unfailingly slots it home.

Born on 20 February 1940 in Bow, London, Greaves made his League debut in 1957 for Chelsea at Tottenham, and scored what became a typical goal, leaving four men tackling air as he calmly slipped in the equaliser. This goal also foretold another happy knack – he never played for

Jimmy Greaves, whose 357 League goals were all scored in the First Division.

a new club or at a new level of football without scoring on his debut.

A frail-looking 5 ft 8 in, his acceleration and dainty ball control were devastating, and in his four seasons with Chelsea, with his long and baggy shorts, he looked like a boy making men look silly as he scored goal after goal – three times five in a match, including one inspired afternoon against Billy Wright and his mighty Wolves, and three times four in a match. He then went to AC Milan to seek riches in 1961, but the maximum wage was abolished before he left, and after one season Spurs paid £99,999 to bring him back to England, where he resumed his prodigious goal scoring, becoming Spurs' leading scorer with 220 League goals.

Greaves played 495 Football League matches, and scored 357 goals – all in the First Division, a remarkable record. In all, he scored 492 goals, and was the First Division's top scorer in five seasons. He won two FA Cup winner's medals and a European Cup Winners Cup winner's medal with Spurs, before ending his career with West Ham. He played 57 times for England at inside forward, including three in the World Cup winning side of 1966, when he lost his place through injury. He scored 44 goals for England, second only to Bobby Charlton.

Eddie Hapgood

Bristol Rovers allowed amateur Eddie Hapgood to drift away and join non-League Kettering Town in 1925 – an expensive mistake, because Arsenal signed him in 1927 and he became one of the best full backs the game has seen.

Hapgood's first job was to build strength into his small frame, which he did so well that he played 393 First Division games for the Gunners. He became famous for his skill at full back in an age when full backs generally supplied a side's brawn, and his anticipation led to a reputation for goal-line clearances.

Arsenal were so strong in the 1930s that Hapgood won five Championship and two FA Cup winner's medals. He made his debut for England in 1933, and was made captain in 1934, three years before he was captain of Arsenal. His first match as England captain was in the infamous battle against Italy at Highbury, when Hapgood, who returned after having his nose broken, had six Arsenal colleagues in the side which beat the World Cup holders 3-2. In 1939 he led England to victory at Hampden Park, the first win there for 12 years.

His England career was cut short by the war, when he had 30 caps – then a record. He played 13 more times in wartime internationals, and was captain in all 34 times. He loved Arsenal, and was disappointed when football could not use his talents to the full after his retirement. He died in 1973, aged 62.

Johnny Haynes

A one-club man, Johnny Haynes' vision at inside left made him the greatest exponent of the defence-splitting through-pass the game has seen.

He was born on 17 October 1934, and in 1950 amazed England's television viewers with a precocious display in a schoolboy international at Wembley. Quickly signed by Fulham, he made his debut at 18, and played for England at 20.

From his first appearance for Fulham, Haynes controlled every match he played from around the centre circle, treating such internationals as Bedford Jezzard and Bobby Robson almost as his puppets as he slipped them through defences to score. A perfectionist, his apparent impatience with colleagues' misplaced passes sometimes caused criticism, but he made Second Division Fulham's forward line the most exciting in the country. On the abolition of the maximum wage, chairman Tommy Trinder made Haynes Britain's first £100 per week footballer. In all, he played a record 594 League matches for his club.

By the time he was 20 Haynes had

Eddie Hapgood, captain of England, who had a record number of caps when war came to interrupt his career.

Johnny Haynes, the supreme distributor from mid-field, captain and goal-maker of Fulham and England.

become the first man to play for England at schoolboy, youth, Under-23, B and Full International level. He played 56 times for his country, including appearances in the 1958 and 1962 World Cup final tournaments, and was captain 22 times. A car crash ended his international career, but he continued with Fulham to complete 18 years at the club.

Pat Jennings

The toughness of Irishman Pat Jennings is indicated by the fact that he played the rough Gaelic football before joining Newry Town as a goalkeeper, from where he came to Wembley as a 17-year-old in 1963 to shine against England in a European Youth Tournament. Signed by Watford, he played for the full Northern Ireland team before Spurs paid the bargain price of £27,000 to sign him in 1964 as reserve to Scottish international Bill Brown.

Born on 12 June 1945 in Newry, Jennings is said to have the largest hands in soccer, a fact which helps him to make spectacular one-handed saves. His bravery and dependability make him an inspiring last line of defence for any team.

He won an FA Cup winner's medal with Spurs in 1967. In 1977, when he should have been near the end of a distinguished career, Spurs made the apparent mistake of allowing him to go to rivals Arsenal, where he performed as well as ever and won a second FA Cup winner's medal in 1979.

An outstanding feat was to score from a goal kick in the Charity Shield match in 1967 – one of only five instances recorded. He was Footballer of the Year in 1973.

An automatic first-choice goalkeeper for Northern Ireland since 1964, Jennings at the end of the 1979-80 season had a record 83 caps for his country.

Kevin Keegan

Kevin Keegan has made of his soccer prowess a fabulously wealthy business, and the money he has made might be counted as a measure of his charisma and skill. His riches have led some to devalue his football, and he himself is modest about his talents, but he has made the most of his virtues of speed, effort and enthusiasm that he ranks with the best.

Keegan was born on 15 February 1951 in Armthorpe, and spent his years from 17 to 20 unnoticed in Scunthorpe's first team – unnoticed that is except by Bill Shankly

Opposite *Pat Jennings, who had a successful 10-year career with Spurs and then began another one with neighbours Arsenal.*

Left *The World Cup final of 1978, and the man of the tournament, Mario Kempes, with the ball under control.*

Below *Kevin Keegan flicks on the ball in typical fashion for Southampton in 1980-81.*

who bought him ('robbery with violence' he called it) for £35,000 for Liverpool in 1971. Keegan became the darling of the Kop as he was dominant at inside forward in Liverpool's run of successes in the 1970s. He picked up Championship medals in 1973, 1976 and 1977, a Cup winner's medal in 1974, UEFA Cup winner's medals in 1973 and 1976 and a European Cup winner's medal in 1977. He made his debut for England in 1973 and became captain in 1976. He was Footballer of the Year in 1976.

He then expressed a desire to play in Europe, and Hamburg secured his signature on 3 June 1977 for £500,000. He was an instant success, winning a German Championship medal in 1979, and being voted European Footballer of the Year in 1978 and 1979. He continued to play for England and enlarge his sponsorship and endorsement interests. Lawrie McMenemy brought off a coup by signing Keegan for Southampton in the summer of 1980, by which time Kevin had played 54 times for England.

Mario Kempes

Argentina won the World Cup of 1978 on their own grounds playing exciting attacking football, and the spearhead of the attack and top scorer in the tournament was Mario Kempes.

Born on 15 July 1954 in Bell Ville, Argentina, he played for the Instituto de

Cordoba side with his friend Ardiles, before joining Rosario Central with whom he won Argentine Championship medals in 1971 and 1973. In 1976, as Argentina's top scorer, he went to Europe to join Valencia in Spain. He was top scorer in his first two seasons, and won a Spanish Cup winner's medal in 1979 and a European Cup Winners Cup winner's medal in 1980 when Valencia beat Arsenal on penalties.

Like his fellow-countryman and centre forward, di Stefano, he likes to play wherever the ball is and is constantly involved in the play. He played for Argentina in the World Cup in 1974, without scoring, but his six goals in 1978 earned him the Golden Shoe award as the best player of the tournament. He was also South America's Footballer of the Year. He played for Argentina in the Gold Cup tournament of

national. He went to Manchester City for a record £55,000 in 1960 and a year later went to Torino in Italy for £100,000 in search of high wages.

In 1962 Sir Matt Busby, a long-time admirer, bought him for Manchester United for £115,000, Britain's first £100,000-plus footballer. His great days came with United, and few will forget his exhilarating display in the 1963 Cup Final.

Law's forte was aggression (at times some said over-aggression) and his speed and daring in the penalty box brought him many thrilling goals. In particular he was famous for his leaping headers when a flick of his neck sent the ball into goal like a bullet. He won Championship medals in 1965 and 1967 and a Cup winner's medal in 1963. He was European Footballer of the Year in 1964. He ended his days back at

Fingers pointing as Denis Law slots home one of his easier goals for Manchester United past Everton's groping Gordon West.

1981, gaining his 33rd cap, and seems sure to be a force at the World Cup finals in Spain in 1982.

Denis Law

Denis Law was born on 24 February 1940 in Aberdeen, and nobody looked less like a world class footballer when as a thin youth with spectacles and a squint he presented himself at Huddersfield Town for a trial in 1955. However at 16 he was in the first team and in 1958, aged 18 years 236 days, he was Scotland's youngest ever inter-

Manchester City. He played 55 times for Scotland, making just one World Cup appearance, against Zaire in 1974. His 30 goals for Scotland are six more than any other Scot's.

Tommy Lawton

It is remarkable that Lancashire has provided the three best examples of the typically British centre forward — big, strong, fearless leaders of the line with thundering shots and cannon-ball headers. The three were Dean, Lawton and Lofthouse.

Born on 6 October 1919 in Bolton, Lawton was scoring goals for Burnley when only 16, and at 17 he was signed by Everton for a record £6,500 to play alongside Dean, whom he eventually replaced at centre forward. With the two together Everton won the Championship in 1939 and Lawton in that last pre-war season played eight times for England, scoring in his first six matches. The war seriously interrupted his career, and his ninth cap was delayed for over seven years. By this time he was playing two seasons with Chelsea, but in 1947 Notts County of the Third Division paid a record £20,000 for him. He then had a spell as player-manager with Brentford, before ending his career where he belonged, at the top with Arsenal.

Despite the war, he played in 390 League games, scoring 231 goals. He played 23 times for England, scoring 22 goals. Including unofficial wartime and victory internationals he scored 46 goals in 45 matches, and this average of over a goal a game indicates that, but for the war, his record could have been unsurpassed.

Diego Maradona

Although he had been in the original 40-man and 25-man squads, Diego Maradona at 17 was considered too young to play for Argentina in the World Cup of 1978. In the next two years he flashed upon the soccer world, which, hungry for outstanding heroes, soon began to call him the new Pelé.

He first attracted worldwide notice in 1979 by playing outstanding football in Argentina's victory in the Junior World Cup. In 1980 he was, unsurprisingly, South America's Footballer of the Year. On May 13, at Wembley, he played brilliantly against England, causing Ron Greenwood to describe him as 'a bit special'. It was then thought that Barcelona were willing to pay a record $6 million for him, with another $1 m for Maradona. It seemed a deal would go through, but the Argentine FA stepped in with a ban on foreign transfers and a loan of $400,000 to Maradona's small club, Argentinos Juniors, to pay him for the rest of the year. Argentinos Juniors stated Maradona would stay in Argentina until the 1982 World Cup.

In 1980 Argentinos Juniors finished second in Argentina's First Division, and Maradona, with 25 goals, was the League's top scorer for the second year. Since 1976

he had scored 101 goals in 154 matches.

Maradona was born in October 1960, and played in the Gold Cup tournament in Uruguay in 1981, where he earned his 24th cap while still only 20. He plays as a midfield attacker for Argentina, dazzling with his speed and footwork, making and scoring goals. In 1981 Boca Juniors signed Maradona on loan for the 16 months prior to the World Cup. The deal was estimated to cost them about $8 million (nearly £4 m) plus the transfer or loan of six players. Maradona's share was about $2 million. Barring accidents he should make the international scene in the 1980s exciting to watch.

Stanley Matthews

In the days when British football was still universally considered the best, Stanley

Stanley Matthews playing for Blackpool in his third decade of League soccer, with only another ten seasons to go.

Top *The sensation of the 1980s, Diego Maradona of Argentina, beating a Scottish player.*

Above *Bobby Moore guarding West Ham's near post against Leeds in 1973.*

control from the wing later earned him a title of his own, 'The Wizard of Dribble'.

He made his debut for Stoke City in 1931. In 1964-65, aged nearly 50, he played his last game, also for Stoke City, in the First Division. Of such a long career it is possible to give only a few highlights: the astonishing 3,000-strong public protest meeting when he asked for a transfer in 1937; the part he played in England's 6-3 victory over Germany in Hitler's Berlin in 1938 when the players were forced to give the Nazi salute; the romantic Cup final of 1953, 'Matthews' Match', when he turned it on in the last 20 minutes to enable his second club, Blackpool, to come from 1-3 and win 4-3 with two in the last two minutes; the return to Second Division Stoke in 1961 which quadrupled the season's best gate, and where he scored a rare goal in the last match of the next season to ensure promotion; his last cap, aged 46; and the testimonial match in April 1965, when, over 50, he played well against the world's new crop of stars.

Matthews played 698 League matches. He was sometimes thought too individualist for England, and won only 54 caps, plus 26 in wartime and victory internationals. He was Footballer of the Year in 1948 and 1963 (when 48!) and European Footballer of the Year in 1956. He was knighted in 1965. He went to live in Malta, where aficionados could still watch this remarkable man play football.

Bobby Moore

In a career which saw him play 1,000 senior games, Bobby Moore collected honours almost as if by right. Nominally a left half, he was one of the greatest defenders of all time: strong in the tackle, with good constructive vision, and as a natural leader, a captain who inspired the teams he led.

Born on 12 April 1941 in Barking, he was outstanding from a schoolboy, and played a record 19 times for England's Youth team. He joined West Ham United from school, and in 1964 led them to a Cup final victory and in 1965 to a European Cup Winners Cup victory. Having made his debut for England in 1962, he was at Wembley for the third year running in 1966 for his greatest victory of all, captaining England's World Cup winning team and earning the Player of the Tournament accolade.

He attracted publicity, and just before

Matthews was the most famous player in the world.

Supreme fitness ensured a long career for him. Born on 1 February 1915 at Hanley, Staffordshire, he was the son of a well-known boxer, 'The Fighting Barber of Hanley'. A precocious goal-scoring schoolboy (from centre half!) his supreme ball the Mexico World Cup of 1970, he was charged with stealing a bracelet in Bogota. The charge was later squashed, but was hanging over him during the World Cup, where he nevertheless again played brilliantly and confirmed his reputation (with Pelé's endorsement) as the world's best defender.

Before ending his career with Fulham (and another Cup final appearance, ironically against West Ham) he notched up a record 108 caps for England and was England's youngest-ever captain at a month over 22. Blond, handsome and with a model for a wife, he was an advertiser's dream, and reaching the top just as the maximum wage was abolished, he brought

for strong headers. It is easy to see why he scored so many goals.

His international goal-scoring record is tremendous. He four times scored four (against Albania, Cyprus, Russia and Switzerland) as well as four hat-tricks. He scored to end Scotland's chance of getting to the Mexico World Cup finals, and in Mexico scored the winner to knock out holders England in the quarter-finals.

His last goal was the winner in the World Cup final of 1974. He ended with 68 goals in 62 internationals – 14 in World Cup final tournaments, a record. Muller joined Bayern Munich in 1963, and won four Championship medals, three Cup winner's medals, three European Cup winner's

A smile from the greatest of them all – Pelé.

a new trendy image to footballers. He was Footballer of the Year in 1964.

Gerd Muller

Centre forwards do not have to be big. One of the best-ever, Hughie Gallacher, was 5 ft 5 in tall and Gerd Muller is hardly any taller. His physique is remarkable. His legs seem too short, even for a short man, but his calf muscles are like footballs and his thighs like tree trunks. These short strong legs give him a low centre of gravity, allowing close control and quick turning in the penalty box, and they also launch him into the air

medals, one European Cup Winners Cup winner's medal, and a World Club Championship medal. He won, with West Germany, World Cup and European Championship winner's medals. He was European Footballer of the Year in 1970.

Pelé

Edson Arantes do Nascimento was born a poor black boy in Tres Coracoes (Three Hearts), Brazil on 21 October 1940. Thirty years later his adopted name, Pelé, was famous throughout the world – most people's choice as the greatest footballer

Two of the best players in West Germany's successful run in the 1970s, defender Franz Beckenbauer on the left and attacker Gerd Muller, on the right, playing against Russia in the 1972 Nations Cup final.

there had ever been in the history of soccer.

There was no aspect of soccer of which Pelé was not the master. Recommended to Santos at 16, he was in Brazil's World Cup winning team of 1958, aged 17, and announced his arrival with one of the best goals the world has seen in the final. Despite his successes with Santos (nine São Paulo League Championship medals, four Brazilian Cup winner's medals, two South American Cup winner's medals and two World Club Championship medals) it was on the international stage, and particularly in the World Cup, that he stamped his brilliance. He won a winner's medal in 1958, was injured while Brazil won again in 1962, was shamefully kicked out of the

Ferenc Puskas completing an English humiliation as he scores the seventh goal in the 1954 international in Hungary – the thirteenth Hungarian goal in two matches against England.

competition in 1966, but in the sympathetic atmosphere of Mexico in 1970 produced his greatest form when Brazil won again. It is no coincidence that his emergence began Brazil's post-war ascendancy in world football.

It was his style, as well as his mastery, that made him so exciting. Quick, lithe, athletic, infectiously keen, he had a talent for the unexpected. In 1970 it seemed he could do anything, and as if he wanted to bow out with an outrageous touch of genius, he attempted a shot from Brazil's half of the centre circle when Czechoslovakia's great goalkeeper Viktor had advanced too far from his line. It beat the goalie but went a yard past the post. It was a moment of magic that millions of television viewers will treasure of him.

In 1975, when he had already retired, Cosmos of New York gave him a $5 million

contract for three years, and he did much to put soccer on the map in the United States, as is shown by the fact that 77,691 saw his last game for them. In all forms of football, he scored over 1,200 goals, including 97 in 110 matches for Brazil. With his businesses, he became a dollar multi-millionaire, but perhaps he is proudest of the street named after him and the statue unveiled in 1971 in his home town.

Ferenc Puskas

Hungary finally destroyed the illusions of British soccer supremacy on a grey day at Wembley in November 1953, and the man the fans took to their hearts as the image of the new masters was a chubby swaggering jovial inside left with an educated left foot – Ferenc Puskas. From the army side of Honved, he became known as 'The Galloping Major'. One of the goals he scored in that 6-3 massacre was magic – completely diddling Wright and lashing the ball home.

Born on 2 April 1926, he made his international debut aged 17, and Hungary in the early 1950s became the best team in the world. The Hungarian uprising in 1956 stopped all that. Puskas was reported killed, but in fact found his way to Spain, where eventually he joined Real Madrid, to begin a second remarkable career.

Puskas was a midfield general who organised most of the sides for which he played, but he also had a tremendous left foot shot, which brought him hundreds of goals. He won five Championship medals in Hungary and five in Spain, a Spanish Cup winner's medal, a European Cup winner's medal (he scored four in the 1960 final, and three in the lost final of 1962), a World Club Championship medal and an Olympic Gold medal in 1952. He was leading scorer in four seasons in Hungary, and four in Spain. In his international career, he averaged over a goal a game for Hungary – 85 in 84 matches, and he also played four times for Spain.

Bert Trautmann

It is strange that a man who did not play for his country should be included in a gallery of greats, but Bert Trautmann's was a strange career.

He was born on 22 October 1923 in Bremen, Germany, just in time to become a paratrooper in the Second World War. Captured by the British, he played football in a prisoner-of-war camp in Lancashire. After the war he did not return to Germany. He kept goal as an amateur for St Helens, and was spotted by Manchester City, for whom he made his debut in 1949.

Tall, well-built, athletic and full of courage, he became a charismatic goal-keeper. With his blond hair he looked like a lion as he prowled the penalty area and sprang to make saves. After helping City into the First Division in 1951, he was on the losing side in the 1955 Cup final, but was back at Wembley in 1956, becoming Footballer of the Year just before the final. City beat Birmingham 3-1, and Traut-mann played the last 15 minutes in great pain, after diving at the feet of a Birmingham forward. At the end he was helped off clutching his neck, but it was some time afterwards before it was discovered that he had been playing with his neck broken.

Trautmann was not picked by West Germany, and his only representative match was for the Football League against the Irish League in 1960. But nobody who saw a few of his then record 541 League and Cup matches for Manchester City between 1949 and 1956 doubts that he was among the very best goalkeepers.

Billy Wright

Imagine Barbara Cartland writing a novel about a soccer hero, and you have a synopsis for the career of Billy Wright. Rejected at 15 by Wolves for being too small, he broke his ankle when given a second chance, but was allowed to stay as a sweeper-up on the ground staff. Then came the war, and after it a succession of triumphs: captain of Wolves and England, winner of three Championships and a Cup winner's medal, and the first man in the world to play 100 times for his country. And afterwards being awarded the CBE, marrying Joy Beverley, a famous singer, managing the most glamorous club in the world, Arsenal, and then becoming a television executive.

Yet Wright's personality was quite wrong for a steamy romantic role: straight as a die, with an honest face and toothy smile, he was a first-rate team man, with no tantrums and no heroics, just a simple boyish enthusiasm for the game and a pride in playing for England.

He began as a wing half, and switched midway through his career to centre half. Dependability was his forte, especially when the move to the centre curbed his attacking inclinations. Quick and strong in the tackle, good in the air, he covered his colleagues and used the ball simply and well – no frills, no flap.

It earned him respect and admiration: 6,000 turned up at his 'quiet' wedding, 20,000 said their farewells at his last match in 1959, a pre-season trial for his only club, Wolves. Then straight to the top management job – at Highbury. Here, at last, he failed. He was too well-liked in a job where ruthlessness is essential. But his 105 caps, 90 as captain, his post of Head of Sport at ATV, his unassailable niche in soccer history, were compensations enough for any man.

Billy Wright, a one-club man, in the gold shirt of Wolves with whom he had a golden career.

The Giant Killers

Peter Arnold

When Yeovil Town beat Sunderland, or Hereford United knock Newcastle United out of the Cup, something more important is happening than a bonanza for 'Match of the Day'. The soccer fan at large might be gleeful at the discomfiture of the giants, everybody will rejoice at the 'glorious uncertainty' of the game, but to the giant-killers themselves their big moment means a big pay-day that usually eases severe

match without a fight on the terraces. Liverpool, Everton and Manchester United have their diehard fans. Following soccer implies, much more than in other sports, an interest in a particular team.

The big clubs find their supporters everywhere. Manchester United have fans who have never been to Manchester. But how many who do not live in Crewe or Doncaster support Alexandra or Rovers?

An honour for a small club. Swindon captain Stan Harland (centre) showing the Wembley fans the Football League Cup, won in 1963.

financial problems.

To the local supporter the win will be a matter of pride and pleasure that might need to keep him going through several seasons of obscurity for his team.

The supporters of small clubs are true supporters of the game, for without them soccer, as it is at present structured, could not survive. Without them there would be no small clubs, and without small clubs the glamour of the big clubs, and the game itself, would be diminished.

Soccer is a partisan game. Rangers and Celtic can hardly play each other in a big

The Cup competitions, of course, provide the opportunities for those fans to celebrate. How must the supporters of Battling Barnsley have felt in 1912, when their side, never higher than third in the Second Division in its whole history before or since, actually lifted the FA Cup?

It is fanciful to imagine that such great successes could occur these days. Since Second Division West Bromwich Albion won the Cup in 1931, only three teams from outside the First Division have won, all recently: Sunderland, Southampton and West Ham United. And with the

possible exception of Southampton, all these were great cup-fighting sides in temporary decline.

In 100 FA Cup competitions 40 different clubs have won, but this spreading of the honours presents a false picture. Nowadays the power is more than ever with the big clubs, as affluence, the five-day week and the widespread ownership of motorcars have meant that fans are able and willing to travel to see the best. The big clubs get richer and stronger, while the small clubs must now be content with the prospect of giant-killing to bring them fleeting glory.

Since 1960 the League Cup has provided a second opportunity for heroics each season, and in 1962 Rochdale reached the final as a Fourth Division club, despite their record in the FA Cup being about the worst of all 92 League clubs, but in those days the competition was not taken too seriously.

Over the years some clubs have built up a reputation for giant-killing. The names of some non-League clubs have become famous for their Cup exploits. The most notable, perhaps, is Yeovil Town, whose tally of League scalps is now in double figures. Bedford Town, who once drew at Highbury, and Bath City have done well, and some non-League clubs' giant-killing feats have helped them eventually to get League membership, principally Peterborough United, Hereford United, and most recently Wigan Athletic and Wimbledon. Pure amateur clubs have sometimes made their

mark: Walthamstow Avenue drew with Manchester United at Trafford Park in 1952-53 after beating Stockport County, and in 1958-59 Tooting and Mitcham United were two up against Nottingham Forest, only to concede a penalty and an own goal to allow Forest a draw – Forest went on to win the Cup.

Five times non-League sides have registered 6-1 defeats of League sides: Walthamstow Avenue over Northampton Town, Barnet over Newport County, Hereford United over Queens Park Rangers, and away from home Wigan Athletic over Carlisle United and, most astonishing, Boston United over Derby County.

In the 1970s Walton and Hersham United won 4-0 at Brighton, who also lost at home to Leatherhead. In 1974-75 non-League Wimbledon won at First Division Burnley, and then held mighty Leeds United to an away draw. Stafford Rangers and Blyth Spartans, who reached the fifth round after winning at Stoke, also attracted attention.

The more humble League sides also had their moments. In 1971-72 Colchester United, a Fourth Division side, beat Leeds United in the fifth round; in 1973-74 Third Division Wrexham reached the sixth round; in 1975-76 Bradford City, from the Fourth Division, also reached the sixth round. In the first season of the 1980s Exeter City reached the sixth round from the Third Division.

So one need not be sorry for the sup-

Dickie Guy, Wimbledon's goalkeeper, touching a shot from Leeds' Terry Yorath wide of the post during Wimbledon's Cup run of 1974-75. Guy also saved a Lorimer penalty.

Play round the Walsall goal during the sensational Cup-tie against the Arsenal.

ARSENAL'S AMAZING CRASH

"Saturday may have been a dream to the small teams in the Cup-ties, but it was something akin to a nightmare for the "big noises."

Walsall led the way and gave the Arsenal the shock of their lives in defeating them by two goals to none.

The Londoners were completely unsettled and their craft failed against the bustle and energy of the Black Country men.

Jack and James tried desperately hard to set the "machine" going, but always the Arsenal found themselves robbed of the ball.

Alsop, Walsall's leading goalscorer, drove the first nail into Arsenal's coffin and Sheppard, with a penalty, completed the job.

The crowd were almost mad with excitement and the players were carried shoulder high off the field. Thus a struggling Third Division team created a sensation of the century.

Brighton and Chesterfield also hit the high-spots. The Southern Third Division side actually ousted Chelsea from the Cup, while the Second Division men astounded Sheffield Wednesday, at Hillsborough, by thoroughly earning a replay.

It is a tall order, but Tottenham have just the type of side that the Albion had in 1930-31.

I will dismiss the other London sides' efforts with: Charlton got lost in the fog against Bolton at the Valley; the Rangers roved at Darlington and missed their way to the fourth round; Corinth bid adieu in a timorous fashion to the advantage of West Ham, and Millwall meet Reading once again because the fog robbed them of success at New Cross when the game was abandoned.

If Folkestone had possessed ten other players with the ability of their twenty-year-old goalkeeper, Goodman, they would be in the Cup now !

This youth, I am told, fielded all manner of shots with the confidence of a veteran until three-quarter-time ; then, just a couple of slips in judgment allowed Luke and Willingham to scrape Huddersfield through.

Huddersfield's attack had almost battered itself to pieces in attempting to beat Goodman, whose work, says my correspondent, alone seemed to have earned a replay.

Newcastle, the Cupholders, are out ! Leeds did the trick at St. James's Park, thanks mainly to a hat-trick by Hydes.

Top *Manchester United versus Walthamstow Avenue was an unlikely fixture in 1952-53. A draw was an unlikelier result. United won the replay at Highbury.*

Above *The Daily Mirror of Monday, 16 January 1933 tells of Arsenal's amazing crash to Walsall.*

porters of the small clubs. When their moment comes, there is no thrill like it. Celtic and Rangers fans might delight in beating each other, but can the umpteenth Championship title really stir the blood? Loyal Liverpool fans have justly enjoyed their team's great successes, but it is hard when early in 1981 they had to wear long faces because Liverpool were only a distant third in the Championship.

Compare this with the euphoria when a small town draws a giant in the Cup.

Perhaps John Motson arrives and a television squad photographs the town hall and the dressing room 'facilities'. A beaming manager turns arithmetician: 'There are eleven of them and eleven of us', and philosopher: 'We've nothing to lose and everything to gain', and optimist: 'Charlie is looking forward to marking Dalglish'.

A few of the big Cup upsets are described in this chapter. If it seems cruel on the Arsenals and Newcastles, they have one consolation: David would still be an unknown if Goliath had not been a real giant.

Walsall 2 Arsenal 0

The biggest of all Cup shocks occurred on 14 January 1933, when the most powerful team in the world travelled to Walsall for the formality of winning a third round FA Cup-tie. Consider Arsenal. Managed by the great Herbert Chapman, they won the Championship that year, and the following two seasons. In the 1930s alone they won five Championships and two Cups. In 1934 they supplied seven players for England's win over World Cup winners Italy – and they also had Welsh and Scottish internationals. Walsall, on the other hand, before the days of the Fourth Division, seven times had to seek re-election to the Third. Even now their best season was to finish sixth in the Second Division in 1899. One newspaper claimed that Arsenal had £87 worth of football boots, while a season's entire running expenses for Walsall was £75.

Because of 'flu, Arsenal risked three newcomers, but could hardly have expected the shock which came 15 minutes after half-time when Gilbert Alsop headed home a corner for Walsall. It was said the cheers were heard two miles away. Five minutes later Arsenal newcomer Tommy Black conceded a penalty from which Sheppard scored. (After the match, poor Black was transferred to Plymouth, and Arsenal's other newcomers soon left.) In the last 25 minutes Walsall resisted the efforts to score of such great players as Alex James, David Jack and Cliff Bastin, and the Cinderella club from the Black Country had beaten the capital's glamour boys. The Sunday papers had a field day.

Walsall: Cunningham, Bird, Bennett, Reid, Lesley, Salt, Coward, Ball, Alsop, Sheppard, Lee.

Arsenal: Moss, Male, Black, Hill, Roberts, Sidey, Warnes, Jack, Walsh, James, Bastin.

Yeovil Town 2 Sunderland 1

In 1948-49 Yeovil Town were near the bottom of the Southern League, but having fought through from the qualifying rounds of the FA Cup, they found themselves with the big clubs in the third round, where they despatched Second Division Bury 3-1 on their famous sloping pitch. In the fourth round they were again at home, but this time to mighty Sunderland, comfortably in the top half of the First Division.

Over 150 journalists were given desks from a local school on which to write their reports of the part-timer's big day. The omens looked bad when winger Hargreaves was injured after 10 minutes. Substitutes were not then allowed, and he remained a passenger. But Yeovil attacked, and after 28 minutes Alec Stock, their player-manager, lashed in a goal. Yeovil had a reserve goalkeeper, who made many fine saves as Sunderland applied the pressure, but unfortunately after 62 minutes he allowed Robinson to tap in a soft equaliser. It was 1-1 at 90 minutes. In the first four post-war seasons extra time was played on the first tie as an economy measure, so Yeovil had another half-hour of home advantage to win the match. They seized their opportunity when the great Len Shackleton made a mistake and Bryant scored. Three minutes from the end the crowd invaded the pitch thinking the match was over, and as mist rolled down they were cleared only just in time. Yeovil's motley heroes were too exhausted to celebrate. They lost 8-0 to Manchester United in the next round, but their day of glory drew 81,561 to Manchester to watch them.
Yeovil Town: Dyke, Hickman, Davis, Keeton, Blizzard, Collins, Hamilton, Stock, Bryant, Wright, Hargreaves.
Sunderland: Mapson, Stelling, Ramsden, Watson, Hall, Wright, Duns, Robinson, Turnbull, Shackleton, Reynolds.

West Bromwich Albion 2 Port Vale 1

Although Port Vale, champions of the Third Division (North) lost an FA Cup semi-final to the eventual winners West Bromwich Albion in 1954, they came close to creating a record – the first Third Division side to reach Wembley. Port Vale had a magnificent defence that season. Having reached the third round they won 1-0 at Queens Park Rangers; in the fourth they won 2-0 at Cardiff; in the fifth they beat Cup-holders Blackpool, Stanley Matthews included, 2-0; and in the sixth they won 1-0 at Leyton Orient. In the League they conceded only 21 goals in 46 matches, a record until beaten by Liverpool in 1978-79.

West Brom were attempting the Cup and League double, considered at the time impossible. In the semi-final at Villa Park they hurled everything at Port Vale's defence with the same lack of success as less distinguished sides. Three minutes before half-time Vale slipped upfield and Leake scored. In the second half West Brom seemed to be losing heart when a deflection allowed Dudley to equalise in the 66th minute. Four minutes later Lee was brought down on the edge of the penalty area. Despite Vale's view that the foul was outside, the referee gave a penalty. Ronnie Allen, a former Vale player, scored, and Port Vale's great run was ended. No other Third Division club had come so near to Wembley.
West Bromwich Albion: Heath, Rickaby, Millard, Dudley, Dugdale, Barlow, Griffin, Ryan, Allen, Nicholls, Lee.
Port Vale: King, Turner, Potts, Mullward, Cheadle, Sproson, Askey, Leake, Hayward, Tomkinson, Cunliffe.

Norwich City 1 Tottenham Hotspur 0

Norwich City first entered the First Division in 1972, and are now no strangers to the top flight, but as recently as 1959 they were very much a struggling Third Division side, having spent most of their history in the lowest divisions. But a 3-0 defeat of Manchester United, Championship runners-up, in the FA Cup third round inspired out of nowhere one of the great Cup runs of modern times. They despatched Cardiff in the fourth round, but were drawn at White Hart Lane in the fifth, against a Spurs side two years away from their famous double. Cup fever had seized Norwich, and 20,000 supporters went to Tottenham, more than their usual home gate. They saw Norwich lead and Cliff Jones volley a last-minute equaliser for Spurs.

Then came the great night at Norwich, where 38,000 fans sang anthems and cheered on the Canaries to such effect that Danny Blanchflower was to say he had

Hereford's winner on its way into the net from Ricky George in the famous Cup win in 1972.

heard nothing like it anywhere in the world. It was an even match, but Terry Bly, who in his finest season was developing a habit of grabbing vital goals, slotted one in the 63rd minute, and Norwich fans went mad at what was to prove the winner.

A draw at Sheffield United in the sixth round and another delirious replay victory saw the Canaries in the semi-final, where they drew again first time with Luton Town, but finally went out 1-0 in the replay. They had come as close as Port Vale five years earlier to reaching Wembley from the Third Division, but perhaps the defeat of Spurs was the greatest night of that season's soccer.

Norwich City: Nethercott, Thurlow, Ashman, McCrohan, Butler, Crowe, Crossan, Alcock, Bly, Hill, Brennan.
Tottenham Hotspur: Hollowbread, Baker, Hopkins, Dodge, Norman, Iley, Medwin, Blanchflower, Smith, Clayton, Jones.

Hereford United 2 Newcastle United 1

When non-League Hereford United earned a 2-2 draw in the third round of the FA Cup at Newcastle, the country applauded, but did not expect Newcastle to make a mistake in the replay. However several postponements due to the weather caused Cup fever to build in Hereford, and nerves to get to Newcastle. On 5 February 1972 the town, the press and television turned out to see the match. It was well television cameras were there, for they recorded the goal of that or many a season.

Newcastle, if truth were told, were the better side and created all the chances, but squandered them, Malcolm Macdonald in particular missing two easy goals.

However Macdonald nodded home in typical leaping fashion eight minutes from time, and that seemed to be that. Hereford needed a near-miracle, and, breathtakingly, four minutes from the end it came. Ron Radford picked himself up from a tackle, stumbled forwards, took a return pass, and from fully 30 yards hit the most powerful spectacular goal past McFaul. The crowd flooded the pitch, and the team were inspired. The extra time winning cross-shot from substitute Ricky George seemed almost inevitable. Hereford became the first non-League side to beat a First Division club since Yeovil 23 years before. In the next round they took West Ham to a replay (they beat them two years later). The win earned Hereford immediate League status, and in their first season they won promotion and reached the Second Division three years after that.

Hereford United: Potter, Griffiths (George), Mallender, Jones, McLaughlin, Addison, Gough, Tyler, Meadows, Owen, Radford.
Newcastle United: McFaul, Craig, Clark, Nattrass, Howard, Moncur, Busby, Green, Macdonald, Tudor, Hibbitt.

Colchester United 3 Leeds United 2

Colchester United joined the Football League in 1950. They have never yet reached the Second Division. In 1971 they were firmly in the Fourth, but found themselves in the FA Cup fifth round playing Leeds United, all but one an international, the most successful side in the country. Nobody gave them a chance.

However, a foolish hope was born after 17 minutes when 34-year-old Ray Crawford, one of six Colchester veterans seeing out their days in the Fourth Division, headed in a free-kick. Before half-time Crawford got another. On the floor with Reaney after a tackle, as Sprake came out to collect the ball and Charlton thundered in, he stuck out a leg and the ball found the net. If 2-0 was a sensation on half-time boards all round the country, more was to follow. Ten minutes after the interval a long speculative ball from the right dropped perfectly over Charlton and as Sprake stood stranded Simmons headed in. Leeds were in complete disarray, but they were not a near-perfect football machine for nothing, and they came back with their own brand of controlled possession play. Norman Hunter scored after an hour,

Johnny Giles reduced the deficit further, and three minutes from time Mick Jones nearly equalised, but Graham Smith, a hero throughout, saved well. On the greatest day in their history, Colchester had gone as far in the FA Cup as any Fourth Division side – the sixth round. There reality re-asserted itself, and Everton beat them 5-0, a score which highlighted the sheer improbability of the result against Leeds.

Colchester United: Smith, Hall, Cram, Gilchrist, Garvey, Kurila, Lewis, Simmons, Mahon, Crawford, Gibbs.
Leeds United: Sprake, Reaney, Cooper, Bates, Charlton, Hunter, Lorimer, Clarke, Jones, Giles, Madeley.

Swindon Town 3 Arsenal 1

By 1969 Swindon Town had never won an honour, never climbed higher than fifth in the Second Division, and as they battled for promotion from the Third Division prospects of an honour seemed remote for many seasons to come. But the Football League Cup changed all that. They beat Torquay United, Bradford City, Blackburn Rovers, Coventry City, Derby County, and Burnley (after three matches). They had struggled, but they were at Wembley on 15 March 1969 to face mighty Arsenal in the final.

Swindon had a Welsh international in full back Rod Thomas and a loyal winger of great flair in Don Rogers, who was the target of the top clubs for years, but few considered Arsenal were in danger. Most experts had failed to consider the pitch, which after continuous rain was a mixture of mud and sand. Arsenal mistakenly tried to play football on it; Swindon relied on Third Division clear-anywhere chase-everything tactics. It paid off after 35 minutes when Ure made a bad back pass and Smart nipped in to score.

Arsenal piled on the pressure without ceasing, and their football was rewarded at last four minutes from time, when Downsborough, who had played magnificently, dashed out, missed the ball, and allowed Gould to tap home. Psychologically, Arsenal should have had the lift required to win in extra time, but their tremendous efforts through the mud had sapped their energy. It was enough for Don Rogers to take a hand. Just before the extra time interval, some neat jugglery allowed him to shoot home, and in the last minute he broke away from the half-way line, ploughed through the mud, swerved past Bob Wilson and cracked in the clincher. At last the Third Division side had a pot on the sideboard.

Swindon Town: Downsborough, Thomas, Trollope, Butler, Burrows, Harland, Heath, Smart, Smith, Noble, Rogers.
Arsenal: Wilson, Storey, McNab, McLintock, Ure, Simpson, Radford, Sammels, Court, Gould, Armstrong.

Ray Crawford (dark shirt, centre) flicks his head and Colchester United are on their way to the astonishing victory over Leeds United in 1971.

Noble of Swindon rounds the grounded Simpson of Arsenal as Wilson, the Arsenal goalie, comes out to meet the threat. Seconds later Swindon were a goal up through Smart.

A Century of Cup Finals

Martin Tyler

The 98th final of the Football Association Challenge Cup gave me a first-hand insight into the fluctuating drama of the climax to this captivating competition.

For the first time I had been invited by Independent Television to interview the players immediately they left the pitch. In order to comply with the technicalities of the medium, I had to be at my post a quarter of an hour before the final whistle, in the interview area above the dressing-rooms, far removed from any direct view of

one of Wembley's most superbly constructed solo goals. Now my original questions had to be scrapped, but at least I would have extra time to compose the new theme to the interviews. That was a consoling thought that lasted the time it took for Arsenal to kick off; for Liam Brady to prod the ball through to Graham Rix; for Alan Sunderland to thrust out his right leg.

Arsenal now would still be coming up to the interview area with the FA Cup. But the story had developed in its complexity.

The Arsenal winner in the 1979 Cup final. Three goals in the last four minutes meant problems for the television interviewer but excitement for the fans.

what was happening on the playing area.

The only communication with the events of the game was a television screen, and that appeared to afford no problems. Arsenal led Manchester United by two goals to nil. The match was telling a straightforward story. For an interviewer the questions formed easily in the mind. Even easier, it seemed, when Gordon McQueen, four minutes from time, gave Manchester United the consolation of a goal. Their players, I thought, would now be happier to come and share their observations with millions.

All semblance of order, however, disappeared when Sammy McIlroy produced

The interviewer would be as breathless as the players, as those who had watched an historic five minutes, either in the temple of the competition itself or on the television screens. Even in an age when football was being assaulted by jaundiced and cynical appraisal, the FA Cup final had retained its sense of romance. The names of new heroes were being added to a roll of honour that began back in 1872.

The Cup that Pat Rice brandished so proudly in 1979 is the third in the tournament's history. The present trophy was designed in Bradford, and won remarkably for the first time by Bradford City in 1911; the change had been necessitated by the lack of copyright on the second FA Cup, the style of which had been copied in replica and sold to the benefit of privateers.

The original trophy, costing little more than £20, had been created in 1871, but did not survive Aston Villa's winning of it in 1895. Displayed in the shop window of a local boot manufacturer, it was stolen and never recovered.

The first FA Cup final set the tone for competition, the Royal Engineers, 4-7 favourites, losing to the Wanderers. The name of 'A H Chequer' was recorded as the scorer of the game's only goal, later revealed as a pseudonym for M P Betts, one of the FA Committee men who had responded enthusiastically to the proposal from the secretary, Charles Alcock: "that it is desirable that a Challenge Cup should be established in connection with the Association for which all clubs belonging to the Association should be invited to compete."

Fifteen clubs comprised the initial entry,

two of which, Donington School, Spalding, and Reigate Priory, subsequently scratched. The rest came from the south with the exception of Queen's Park from Glasgow, who reached the semi-finals through byes and a walk-over. Their first match brought the Scottish club to London to meet the Wanderers, but after a draw Queen's Park withdrew because they were unable to raise the funds to travel south again for the replay.

Thus the Wanderers moved into the final at Kennington Oval where their 1-0 victory was watched by a crowd of 2,000, regarded as disappointing but explained by contemporary reports as the product of an excessive price of admittance of one shilling! Down the years, particularly before the advent of substitutes, used in the competition for the first time in the 1966-67 season, FA Cup finals have been blighted from time to time by serious injury. The first final was no exception; the Royal

How The Sporting Life *described the first FA Cup Final in 1872.*

Engineers were hampered from the first ten minutes when Lieutenant Cresswell broke a collar-bone.

The FA Cup began in the era of the amateur. The Wanderers won five of the initial seven competitions. Old Etonians, twice, Royal Engineers, Oxford University, Clapham Rovers and Old Carthusians all lifted 'the little tin idol' before the clubs from the north discovered the way to end the domination of the unpaid player.

Lancashire became the focal point of the northern challenge, and before professionalism was finally legalised in 1885, a number of clubs in the country had attracted skilled players south from Scotland. The writing was on the wall for the amateurs in 1882 when Old Etonians gained such a hard-fought victory over Blackburn Rovers that Lord Kinnaird performed a head stand of joy at the final whistle. The following year, in Kinnaird's last final, Blackburn Olympic took the Cup north for the first time by beating the holders 2-1 after extra time. The balance of power had shifted.

Blackburn Rovers emphasised the point with a hat-trick of successes. In 1884 they beat Queen's Park, the culmination of an initial entry list of 101 clubs, an illustration of the developing growth of the FA Cup. The following year the Glasgow club were again the losing finalists, and by an odd coincidence Brown and Forrest were the Rovers' scorers in both victories. The hat-trick was completed against West Bromwich Albion, but only after a replay at Derby where Brown added a unique threesome of his own by scoring again in a 2-0 victory.

Albion's appearance in the final gave an indication of the game's progress in the Midlands where Aston Villa and Wolverhampton Wanderers, among others, led the upsurge. But Lancashire produced the next milestone in the competition's history with the unparalleled feats of Preston North End in the 1888-89 season. Statistically the record of the 'Invincibles' stands alone; the League Championship won without defeat and the 'double' completed in the FA Cup without conceding a goal. Twenty-two thousand, a record attendance, were attracted to the final where Preston disposed of Wolves by three goals to nil.

That massive gate spelt the beginning of the end for Kennington Oval. It last saw the final in 1892 when West Bromwich Albion beat Aston Villa, the first with goalnets in operation. A switch to Fallowfield, the home of the Manchester Athletic Club, was no improvement in terms of crowd control, and after one further year, at Everton, Crystal Palace offered a regular venue until the outbreak of the First World War.

The finals at Crystal Palace still stand prominently in the hundred years of competition. In 1903, for example, Bury registered what remains the highest margin of victory, putting six goals past Derby County whose goalkeeper, Fryer, was stricken with injury. Three years earlier Bury had overwhelmed Southampton 4-0, thus giving them a memorable record from their only two years of Cup glory.

Southampton reached the final as members of the Southern League, as they were to do again in 1902, when they so narrowly lost to Sheffield United after a replay. So the honour of being the only non-League winners went instead to Tottenham Hotspur, conquerors of Sheffield United in 1901. The progress of this minnow from the Southern League into the mainstream of the competition so captured the public imagination that more than 110,000 crammed into Crystal Palace; drawn, too, by the possibility of a southern success for the first time for eighteen years.

Tottenham did not fail them, but they needed a replay at Bolton to secure the prize. Two goals from Alexander Brown gave Spurs the edge in the first game, but a contentious equaliser by Bennett forced the second meeting. When Priest put Sheffield United in front it seemed that the League pecking order would remain intact. But Cameron equalised and further goals from Lipsham and Brown completed surely the biggest Cup upset of all time.

For sheer excitement and football quality, the 1897 final at Crystal Palace stands apart. Aston Villa had already galloped away with the League Championship, but Everton were to press them hard as Villa sought to emulate Preston's dual triumph eight years earlier. Campbell's opening goal after 18 minutes eased Villa ahead, but ten minutes later they trailed. Bell raced clear to equalise for Everton, then Boyle made the most of a free-kick.

Remarkably Villa reversed the position before half-time. Wheldon and Crabtree produced what turned out to be the final

decided by Freeman's goal early in the second half. For Boyle, the Burnley captain, it was a case of first and last, the first recipient of the FA Cup from the monarchy but the last at a final at Crystal Palace.

Although hostilities had been declared, the 1914-15 competition was played to a finish. Sheffield United beat Chelsea 3-0 at Old Trafford before a crowd of whom so many were in military uniform that the match acquired the reputation of the 'khaki Cup final'.

United held the Cup for five years before Aston Villa won the first of three post-war finals to be held at Stamford Bridge. Huddersfield Town were beaten by one of the luckiest of winning goals, Kirton unwittingly deflecting in Villa's winner from a corner. Two years later Huddersfield returned with more success. Now heavily under the control of the great manager,

One of Aston Villa's three wins at Crystal Palace – Devey of Villa and Higgins of West Brom clash heads.

Cover of an early Wembley Cup final programme – that of 1927, the only year in which the Cup left England.

goals of the game that continued with dramatic twists to its plot to the very last.

If Aston Villa retain happy memories of Crystal Palace – they also were winners there in 1895, 1905 and 1913, in front of a massive following of 120,081 – the same cannot be said of Newcastle United. The very nature of the FA Cup has always made it a breeding ground for ritual and superstition, and Newcastle's experiences in south London in the early years of the twentieth century led to a definite belief in a jinx. Between 1905 and 1911 they reached *five* finals, but despite their prominence at the time only once did they become Cup winners ... and that, in 1910, was at Everton, after their lack of affinity with Crystal Palace had produced only a draw with Second Division Barnsley in the first meeting.

Barnsley, in fact, reached the final again two years later, overcoming West Bromwich Albion. Their success represented a third triumph for Second Division clubs, following Notts County in 1894 and Wolverhampton Wanderers in 1908. Subsequently West Bromwich Albion (1931), Sunderland (1973), Southampton (1976) and West Ham United (1980) added to the non-First Division winners of the competition.

By 1914 the number of entrants had swollen to 476. This was the year that a ruling monarch attended the final for the first time. King George V witnessed a stern encounter between Burnley and Liverpool,

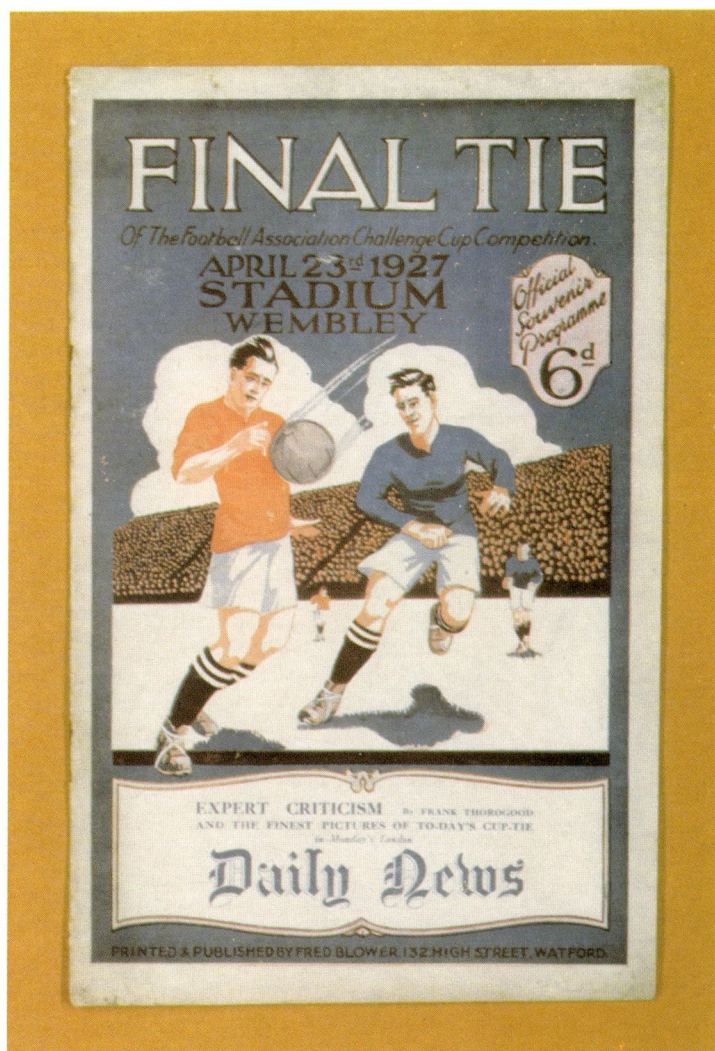

Herbert Chapman, they needed a penalty from Billy Smith to overcome Preston North End.

It was a match that would be mirrored 18 years later. Then Alf Young, the Huddersfield international defender, was adjudged to have brought down George Mutch in the last minute of extra time to give Preston a penalty. Still dazed, Mutch took the kick himself, and struck the underside of the bar before the ball crossed the line for the goal that brought revenge for 1922.

A year earlier Tottenham Hotspur, now rightfully in the First Division, had beaten Wolves with a shot well-struck in boggy conditions by Jimmy Dimmock. Indeed the three finals at Stamford Bridge produced but one goal apiece.

So it was in the 51st year of the FA Cup's history that a new centre entered its life, a home for the final that has become synonymous with the competition. The Empire Stadium, Wembley, was not constructed specifically for football. As its name indicates, the erection of the new arena belonged to the British Empire Exhibition; early in 1922 the removal of a quarter of a million tons of clay followed by the arrival of 1,500 tons of steel and 25,000 tons of concrete confirmed the birth of what has become a footballing dream factory.

Yet the events of 28 April 1923 nearly finished its link with the FA Cup final there and then. Wembley Stadium's history is full of conflict between demand and supply, but never more so as when Bolton Wanderers and West Ham United contested its initial FA Cup final. Crowd estimates vary; the official attendance figure stands at 126,047, but it seems certain that nearer 200,000 crammed into the new edifice. The inevitable consequence of the crush, the spillage onto the pitch, seriously threatened play taking place, but Police Constable George Scorey and his legendary white horse, Billy, played a major role in forcing the crowd back at least beyond the perimeters of the pitch.

No match, before or since, has surely been acted out in such amazing circumstances, with the spectators pressed like commuters in a rush hour right up to the very touchlines. There was barely room for a player taking a corner to swing a leg at the ball, or to stay off the pitch to take a throw-in correctly. Thankfully the age of the pitch invasions was a long time away, and a sense of discipline prevailed, especially remarkable when Bolton took the lead inside two minutes.

David Jack confirmed his place in the story of FA Cup finals with the first Wembley goal, and Bolton went on to win 2-0. They would win again in 1926, with another Jack goal against Manchester City, and in 1929 against Portsmouth. Dick Pym kept his goal intact in all three finals, and along with Haworth, Nuttall, Seddon and Butler won a hat-trick of medals. David Jack obtained his third success with Arsenal in their 1930 win over Huddersfield Town.

Three years earlier Arsenal had been on the wrong end of another piece of Cup final history. Cardiff City's defeat by Sheffield

Constable George Scorey and his conspicuous white horse Billy, who became famous for helping to clear the pitch before the 1923 Cup final, Wembley's first.

United in 1925 had already marked them as the first Welsh finalists, but now they became the only non-English side in the first hundred FA Cup competitions to parade the trophy. As the game moved into the final quarter of an hour of normal time, Ferguson swung a hopeful long-range shot straight at Lewis in the Arsenal goal. But the ball squirmed under his body and over the line, with the goalkeeper, ironically a Welsh international, blaming the sheen on an unwashed, new jersey for the error.

Arsenal's victory in 1930, which hinged on a moment of inspiration from Alex James, was followed two years later by defeat in controversial circumstances against Newcastle United. The north London club led through a goal from Bob John when Richardson crossed a ball from the right that appeared to have passed over the goal-line. Allen turned the centre into the net and the goal was given as an equaliser. Newcastle went on to win 2-1, with Allen also scoring the winner. However, film and photographic coverage suggested that the referee, W P Harper from Worcester, did err in allowing Allen's first goal to stand. But Arsenal would win again before the Second World War; that gallant forward Ted Drake hitting a left-footed deciding goal against Sheffield United in 1936.

Two years earlier Manchester City had bounced back from defeat by Everton, with Dixie Dean and company, in the 1933 final, to return victorious the following year. In City's goal the 19-year-old Frank Swift passed out with excitement as the final whistle confirmed a 2-1 win over Portsmouth. In 1935, Ellis Rimmer struck twice in the last three minutes to settle a thrilling victory for Sheffield Wednesday over West Bromwich Albion.

The decade ended with the clouds of war darkening the horizon but not before Portsmouth had imprinted another shock on the story of the competition. Wolverhampton Wanderers, the strongest favourites for years, and runners-up in the First Division, were humbled 4-1 by a team that finished 17th in the table. Manager Jack Tinn, of the 'lucky spats', out-psyched his counterpart, another cavalier of the age, Major Frank Buckley.

In the first post-war final, Bert Turner of Charlton Athletic scored for both sides within a minute! But Derby County with the heady combination of Peter Doherty and Raich Carter won 4-1 after extra time.

Presumably because of the poor quality of wartime materials the match ball burst, as it did the following year, but not, as it might easily have done, as a result of Chris Duffy's ferocious volley which brought Charlton success this time, against Burnley.

Manchester United and Blackpool provided six goals, and a match of the highest quality in 1948, but some of the merit in United's 4-2 win has been forgotten. Nowadays that Blackpool defeat, together with another in 1951 through two brilliant Jackie Milburn goals for Newcastle United, is regarded more as one of the preliminaries to Stanley Matthews' Cup final showpiece of 1953.

In Coronation Year Blackpool had reached the final again, providing at 38 a last chance of a winner's medal for the country's most spectacular talent, the Wizard of Dribble. In truth for much of the match Matthews did not play well. Bolton led 3-1 but injuries and a tactical naivety allowed Matthews to make a belated but telling contribution. Stan Mortensen claimed all three of the goals that lifted Blackpool level, the only Wembley Cup final hat-trick, but Matthews captured the headlines by cutting the ball back in injury time for Bill Perry to complete the fairy story.

In the 1950s Newcastle United exhibited a rapport with Wembley that was in total contrast to their earlier lack of ease at Crystal Palace, their victims – Arsenal in 1952, Manchester City in 1955 as well as Blackpool in 1951 – creating a trio of Geordie triumphs. But City survived the

The Manchester United side which won one of the great finals in 1948. The front row consists of the captain, manager and the mercurial forward line: Delaney, Morris, Carey (captain), Busby (manager), Rowley, Pearson and Mitten.

finished, and in 1956 Bert Trautmann, that charismatic goalkeeper, broke his neck in protecting Manchester City's 3-1 win over Birmingham.

There were broken legs, too, for Roy Dwight, after he had opened the scoring for Nottingham Forest in 1959, and Dave Whelan, a loser on all counts with Blackburn Rovers in 1960. Though most of the damaging incidents were accepted as coming within the cut and thrust of the game, there was more doubt about the challenge from Aston Villa's Peter McParland in 1957. His shoulder charge led to Manchester United losing goalkeeper Ray Wood with a broken cheekbone as early as the sixth minute. To add insult to injury McParland scored twice past centre-half Jackie Blanchflower, Wood's stand-in, and

Above Stanley Matthews and Harry Johnston in 1953, the year Stan finally got his winner's medal.

Right One of Wembley's more famous incidents. Manchester City's Bert Trautmann is supported by Dave Ewing after hurting his neck diving at a Birmingham forward's feet in 1956. Trautmann played on, though his neck was later found to be broken.

experience of defeat to return victorious the following year, just as they had done 22 years earlier.

This was the era of the Wembley hoodoo when time after time a Cup final disappointed as a spectacle because of a crucial injury. In 1952 Arsenal battled in vain with ten men as Wally Barnes badly twisted a knee. In 1953 Eric Bell limped on for Bolton and even scored when he was, in the vernacular of the day, 'a passenger'. Two years later Jimmy Meadows damaged a leg so severely that his senior career was

the Busby Babes, favourites for the first twentieth century double, lost 2-1.

There was little sentiment, either, the following year when United battled back to Wembley shorn of the core of their great side by the Munich air tragedy. Bolton Wanderers produced a level-headed performance for a 2-0 success, though the second of Nat Lofthouse's goals would not have survived the scrutiny of today's officials. Lofthouse shouldered goalkeeper Harry Gregg and the ball over the line.

The injury jinx even dampened the

historic season of Tottenham Hotspur, 1960-61, when they accomplished the 'double', a feat that had appeared impossible in the increasing pressure of the modern game. At Wembley Leicester City were showing signs of thwarting Spurs in their quest to add the Cup to their League Championship when Len Chalmers, their right-back, sustained a damaging leg injury. Tottenham finally won 2-0 with goals from Smith and Dyson, but their overall performance was more attractive in their retention of the trophy against Burnley.

Tottenham won again in 1967, in the first twentieth century all-London final, and the first in which substitutes were finally made available. Chelsea, young and fashionable under Tommy Docherty, were their victims. Elsewhere in the 1960s, Denis

Above *The injury hoodoo again. McParland scores for Villa, against makeshift goalie Jackie Blanchflower, and Manchester United's dream of the double in 1957 fades.*

Left *Back at Wembley in 1958, with a new team after the Munich disaster, United went down once more to two goals from Bolton's Nat Lofthouse (white shirt).*

Below *The only replay between the First World War and 1981, and Chelsea's first win as David Webb's header finally sinks Leeds in 1970.*

Above *Charlie George scores a spectacular extra-time winner for Arsenal against Liverpool in 1971.*

Right *Arsenal lose this time as Geoff Barnett is beaten by Allan Clarke's header in the Centenary Final of 1972, to give the Cup to Leeds.*

Another year, and Leeds lose on the roundabout of success. Porterfield scores for Second Division Sunderland.

Law inspired Manchester United in 1963 and West Ham's Ron Boyce popped in a last-minute winner to spoil a proud performance from Second Division Preston North End in the 1964 final. The following year Ian St John twisted into an acrobatic header in extra time to inscribe Liverpool's name for the first time on the competition's roll of honour, and in 1968 Jeff Astle drove in one of Wembley's more spectacular winning goals to settle, again in extra time, a win for West Bromwich Albion over Everton.

Everton had been seeking to repeat their triumph two years earlier when Sheffield Wednesday's Gerry Young trod on the ball to allow Derek Temple to sprint clear and complete a dramatic comeback; Everton had trailed 2-0. But Neil Young of Manchester City had a happier experience in 1969; he fired in a cross from Mike Summerbee to make Leicester City losers for the third time in the decade.

Frank McLintock battled valiantly through all those defeats until a move to Arsenal brought about a remarkable change in fortune. In 1971 Arsenal set out to keep the Cup in London – Chelsea had beaten Leeds United after a replay at Old Trafford the previous year – and more importantly to emulate the achievements of Spurs ten years earlier. McLintock, an enterprising wing half with Leicester, now brought leadership and defensive stability to Arsenal as a centre half, but he must have felt that fate was to be against him again when early in extra time Arsenal went behind to Liverpool.

But Arsenal's duel with Leeds for the League Championship had been characterised by dogged refusal to accept defeat, and goals from Kelly and George sent McLintock up to the Royal Box to get his hands at last on the FA Cup.

Arsenal failed to retain the trophy, losing 1-0 to Leeds United in the Centenary final, and Leeds in their turn were beaten as they looked for a second successive win. In 1973 their side shimmered with internationals, and on paper carried far too much weight for Sunderland, who had spent the first half of the season struggling to avoid relegation to the Third Division. But Bob Stokoe, a Cup winner as a player with Newcastle in

Above *Roger Osborne's great moment as he hammers in Ipswich's winner against Arsenal in 1978.*

Left *Trevor Brooking on the floor after getting his head to Pearson's misdirected shot and beating Arsenal's Jennings and goal-line defenders in 1980.*

The goal which seemed for a minute to have won the Cup for Manchester United in 1979. Sammy McIlroy's late equaliser, which was promptly cancelled out by Alan Sunderland's winner.

Paul Allen, of Second Division West Ham, winners in 1980, is the youngest player to have been in a Wembley final. Arsenal's Brady, coming to challenge, was the star of the 1979 final.

1955, brought about a transformation and Sunderland played out the role of underdog in fairytale style. Jimmy Montgomery's instinctive save from Peter Lorimer did most to protect a lead provided by Ian Porterfield's goal.

Manchester United fell in similar style in 1976 to Southampton, whose Second Division players included the likes of Mick Channon and Peter Osgood, talents that sprang to life for the big occasion. The honour of the decisive goal went to one of the lesser names, the modest Bobby Stokes, who blushingly admitted that he could not drive the car that was presented to the game's match winner.

United happily wore the mantle of underdog themselves the following year,

catching Liverpool in the middle of a treble quest for the League, FA Cup and European Cup. United won 2-1, their only major trophy in the 1970s.

The next three years provided a switchback of emotions for Arsenal, the first side to reach three consecutive Wembley finals. In 1978 they came a poor second to Ipswich Town, whose refreshing approach to their first final should have brought a greater margin of victory than the one goal from Roger Osborne. The scorer was so overcome that he had to be substituted for the game's remaining 13 minutes.

The dramas of 1979 brought Arsenal success in that memorable finale against Manchester United, and Brian Talbot, a winner with Ipswich, added a second medal. Talbot returned for a third year as Arsenal met Second Division opposition in their bid to keep the trophy at Highbury.

West Ham United ruined the hat-trick, however, by hanging on to a rare header from Trevor Brooking, a goal in the 14th minute. Seventeen-year-old Paul Allen, whose uncle Les had been in the Spurs double side, took the Cup into a new generation, and his tears of joy as he collected his winner's medal epitomised the feel of the entire competition.

Fittingly, two famous Cup-fighting sides fought out the 100th final in 1981, Spurs beating Manchester City, 3-2 after a 1-1 draw, and the Cup began its second glorious century.

European Competitions

John Moynihan

Before the age of the jet plane, and the space age of 1981, in which Brian Clough led the European champions, Nottingham Forest, on a 25-hour round trip to Tokyo to play Nacional of Uruguay in a World Club Championship final, famous soccer clubs moved more slowly, in many cases, enduring hard labour in transit, and travelling by third-class rail, army trucks, or by chilly buses. Travel, then, was an adventure; now it is pure routine – you hardly have to carry a toothbrush these days into Europe on a short trip.

Clough's Japanese quick longhaul must have amused Raich Carter, one of England's most eminent inside forwards of the 1930s and 1940s. Once delayed because of international duty, he found himself penniless in Frankfurt in 1946 while trying to join Derby County, the first post-war FA Cup holders, who were due to play a match in Prague. Later, Carter regretted the enthusiasm shown by the United States Army to get him to the match in time: "It was the worst game I had ever played in and it was just as well that it was the last one of the tour because I would have refused to play in any matches of that type," the former Sunderland wizard reflected later. "The roughness became an open declaration of war in the first half . . ."

Violence has not been curbed in matches between European teams – but the overall, competitive structure has certainly become intrinsically organised since those early post-war years when Carter combed Frankfurt for a lorry to take him east. It took ten years for an official European Cup competition to come into being, and another twenty before the process had settled into the methodic, familiar charting of a train timetable.

In the 1950s, some progressive thinking by European soccer commentators was to alter the course of club soccer on that continent – with aircraft available to transport teams to other countries, it was ob-

vious that some sort of official cup competition was called for. But as the idea became more concrete, the imperial guard of European soccer declined to show enthusiasm–one member, predictably the English Football League, thought such a competition might upset their own divine domestic programme.

Ironically, one of the first teams to urge matters to a head were Wolverhampton Wanderers, the English League Champions, who took on Honved, the giants of

The line-ups before the game that inspired the European Cup, the Wolves versus Honved floodlit friendly on 12 December 1954 Above Wolves, *skipper Wright at left. Below* Honved, *with flowers, Puskas at right.*

Hungary, on a wintry night at Molineux in 1954. The game was billed as a friendly, but was more than that. The Hungarians were in vogue, they had style, the great national team had lost surprisingly to West Germany earlier in the year in the World Cup final in Berne – now Puskas and Kocsis arrived in the Midlands as members of the Honved team, and Wolves were made to fear for their lives. But by the end of a sensational match, it was the gritty, black pudding-spiced football by the English Champions, with Hancocks and Swinburne running wild, which won the day by 3-2. And 55,000 spectators rejoiced.

One of the observers that night was Gabriel Hanot, a former French international, and national team selector. It was Hanot, by now a journalist, who proposed in the French sporting newspaper *L'Equipe* that there was "a strong case for starting a World Championship, or at least, a European Championship of clubs . . ." But although *L'Equipe* eagerly took up the campaign, FIFA, and the European soccer bosses, UEFA, trod water. Too complicated, it seemed.

Hanot and his pioneers were not altogether worried by such a snooty reaction – *L'Equipe* invited representatives of 18 European countries to attend a meeting in Paris to discuss the idea. It was the spring of 1955, and they had 15 acceptances. It was not a prickly meeting – the first European Cup competition, put quickly into motion, took place only months later, with the belated approval of FIFA (who demanded that clubs take part with the approval of their national organisations) and UEFA, who decided that running the competition was better than not running anything at all.

The competition was officially named the European Champion Clubs Cup, and was to be the first of three regular competitions which were to become a feature of European soccer competition from then on – the others being the European Cup Winners Cup, begun in 1960-61, and the Inter-Cities Fairs Cup (later the UEFA Cup) which became an official competition for club sides in 1958. Hanot, the shrewd footballer, turned journalist, had pioneered a grand venture, which, unfortunately, would lead to times of trouble and strife, financial greed, many riots, and a paucity of skills. But overall, the ideas were sound, and great teams born. . . . Football was

geared for the age of the plane – apart from some cautious nations like Russia, who at first said 'Sorry, Niet', and dear old Chelsea Football Club, deprived of an entry in 1955 to the European Cup because of their own caution.

Chelsea had won the 1954-55 League Championship for the first and only time in their history – but despite the enthusiasm of their manager, Ted Drake, for the new project, they bowed out, under pressure from the Football League, from accepting the invitation to enter Europe. It was not until the next decade that they ventured to take part in Fairs Cup competitions, their most memorable achievement being their long run in the 1965-66 season in which they reached the semi-finals before losing to the eventual winners, Barcelona. In an earlier round, Chelsea were victims of a crowd riot when playing AS Roma and the Italian team were fined, and banned from playing in the competition for three years. This was certainly not the last riot seen in European competition.

Chelsea, meanwhile, were to earn their greatest honour outside domestic competition in 1971 when they beat Real Madrid, after a replay in Athens in the European Cup Winners Cup final.

Real had dominated the early era of the European Cup, which has now celebrated its 25th anniversary. With players like di Stefano, Puskas, Del Sol, Kopa and Gento to call on, their wonderfully vivid play and almost arrogant displays monopolised the field in the later part of the 1950s. The run earned them victories in the first five finals, but the most dramatic and enriching was the last of the five on a spring evening at Hampden Park, Glasgow in 1960. Their opponents were Eintracht Frankfurt, no mean side, but although the Germans took the lead, Real thrilled 127,000 spectators with their effortless football. Three goals by di Stefano and four by Puskas, 'The Galloping Major', earned a 7-3 score line for the Spaniards, so persuasive and exciting being the entertainment that the normally fastidious and insular Scottish fans refused to leave the stadium until the Spaniards had done a lap of honour.

This was the truly golden age of the competition – other great teams were to overtake Real like Benfica, Inter Milan, Ajax of Amsterdam and the strong British challenge later led by Glasgow Celtic, Manchester United, Liverpool and

Alfredo di Stefano scoring for Real Madrid in the 1960 European Cup final in Glasgow.

Nottingham Forest, but somehow a sense of unmatched greatness will always be associated with Real's feats. They were rightly called Club Kings of the World, and proved it by convincingly beating Penarol, the South American champions, in a two-leg affair in first World Club Championship bouts in 1961. This dubious instigation got off to a brilliant start with Real in dazzling form in both legs, but in later years, some European Cup holders found their voyages to South America tinged with acid, Manchester United and Celtic both facing crowd troubles on and

Spurs had a good European Cup run in 1962, beating Dukla Prague in the snow at White Hart Lane (above) to reach the semi-final. Bobby Smith is about to put Spurs ahead.

In the semi-final Spurs beat eventual winners Benfica 2-1 at home (left: Greaves getting in a shot) but lost 3-1 in Portugal.

69

off the pitch. Some winners turned down invitations to take part, but Nottingham Forest did respond to the bait by making that long journey to Japan in early 1981, to lose by a goal to Nacional of Uruguay.

That was 24 years after Manchester United had pioneered the way for English clubs entering European competition. Matt Busby, their perceptive manager, had been keen on the European Cup project from the start, and after Manchester United won the Football League Championship in 1956, he was quick to enter his team for the new competition. The United side were already a famous and still maturing one in England – the hallowed 'Busby Babes', blessed with a rich amount of playing talent with players of the class of Byrne, Edwards, Taylor and Jackie Blanchflower in the side.

In the early rounds of the 1956-57 European Cup, Busby's 'Babes' provided strong evidence of their amazing potential – in a memorable match at Old Trafford, Anderlecht of Brussels were routed by ten clear goals, Dennis Viollet scoring four. Subsequently, United came across Real Madrid in a semi-final, and had to bow to the maturer skills of the eventual winners – but their own performances in the two ties showed they were a team emerging, and quite capable of taking over Real's crown, once di Stefano and company decided it was freely available; a challenge, indeed.

But the prospect never flowered. The Munich air crash in February 1958 destroyed a team; Matt Busby survived some terrible injuries, but some of his finest players were lost, Roger Byrne, Tommy Taylor, Duncan Edwards, to name three. United had been on their way back to Manchester after beating Red Star, Belgrade, in a European Cup quarter-final when their Elizabethan plane crashed trying to take off on a snowy runway – a city went into mourning. But the courage and tenacity of Busby's assistants at Old Trafford quickly summoned reserve strength and United, apart from reaching the 1958 FA Cup final (losing 2-0 to Bolton), were able to take part in the European semi-final against AC Milan. They won the first leg 2-1, but were well beaten by 4-0 in the return leg. Milan in the final played remarkably well against Real Madrid, who had to battle with all their distinctive flair to beat the Italians 3-2.

Gento, one of the great matadors of European Cup competition scored the winning goal in extra time with the cheekiest of goals. Manchester United would have to bide their time for European honours, ten long years, in fact, before a new team guided by Crerand, Law, Charlton, who had survived the crash, and a youthful and often elusive genius from Northern Ireland, Best, took their team into the final for the first time. But a British side had been there before them only a year earlier – Jock Stein's Celtic, in part a veteran side with English club rejects like Auld, and the indefatigable Simpson in goal (he had kept for Newcastle United in the 1952 and 1955 FA Cup finals), produced some bonny attacking soccer to reach the final against Inter-Milan in Lisbon and win the trophy wondrously. Mind you, Celtic were quite a side under the strong-willed, no-nonsense Stein – they won the League title that season, scoring 111 goals in 34 games, they took the Scottish Cup, and won the League Cup – but the Inter game was a tricky one. The Italians, with their dreaded smothering carpet defence, had won the European Cup on two occasions, in 1964 and 1965. Real Madrid had made a brief comeback, winning the trophy again against Partizan, Belgrade, in 1966.

Celtic could not complain about the fanatical support which followed them all the way from Glasgow to Lisbon – but despite the Tartan enthusiasm, they went behind through a Mazzola penalty after eight minutes. It took a long, frustrating time to come back and win with late goals scored by Gemmell and Chalmers, blasted, then nicked, past a magnetic-fingered Inter goalkeeper, Sarti. It was a famous victory, and the Scottish fans poured onto the pitch to celebrate. Some, according to witnesses, never returned to their home land, preferring to stay in Portugal, marry and raise families, and on every anniversary of the victory raise a glass of port and chant 'H'way, Stein's bonny Army!'

Celtic had proved to Britain that winning the coveted trophy was possible, despite the demands of domestic football. They proved this again by reaching the final in 1970 when they lost to Feyenoord, not altogether surprisingly because Dutch football was very much on the upgrade. But by now, there was another name on the Cup – Manchester United.

European Cup Winners Cup win for Scotland. Colin Stein of Rangers jumps but Pilgul, the Moscow Dynamo goalkeeper catches in Rangers 3-2 win in 1972.

Below Liverpool's second successive European Cup win in 1978. Kenny Dalglish about to chip the ball for the only goal of the final against Bruges.

71

World Cup stars as Eusebio, the 'Cobra', Coluna, and the towering Torres.

The crowd were behind United from the start, sensing a great night for Sir Matt Busby and his team. Denis Law was not in the side, still recovering in hospital from injury, but players with the experience of Charlton, Crerand, Stiles and Stepney steered United safely out of the furious tempest Benfica put upon them late in normal time, when they equalled a first-half header by Charlton. Eusebio would have won the match then had he not tried to break Stepney's rib cage with time running out. A touch in, and United would have lost – as it was, goals by Best, with a wonderful solo effort, Kidd, and another from Charlton saw United through. It was time for all Old Trafford to celebrate – a long overdue victory earned after many

The European Cup of 1968. Top Manchester United's George Best beats Real Madrid goalkeeper Betancourt in the semi-final.
Below *David Sadler just fails to get to a cross in United's exciting extra time win over Benfica in the final.*

The magic moment occurred at Wembley in 1968 when Benfica were beaten in extra time with George Best rampant. The Portuguese side came to London with an enviable reputation. Twice winners of the trophy, against Barcelona in 1961, and Real Madrid, in a thrilling affair in Amsterdam a year later, which saw Puskas finish on the losing side despite scoring a hat-trick, they could call on such valuable

years of near-misses, not to mention a stunning tragedy.

Nine years later, Liverpool, the most consistent team ever produced in Britain, were to bring the trophy back after a long absence – the early part of the 1970s had been dominated by two teams from Holland and West Germany, Ajax of Amsterdam and Bayern Munich. This was not altogether surprising because Ajax had the services of one Johan Cruyff, one of the most gifted of all footballers, and Bayern were captained by Franz Beckenbauer. Ajax won the trophy three times on the trot, and Bayern afterwards did the same.

With Dutch and West German club football so dominant, the expected South American challenge withered in the 1974 World Cup finals in West Germany with the host nation triumphing in a classic contest in the final against Holland, the winning goal scored by Gerd Muller, who as Bayern's goal-scoring ace, was to contribute much to his side's feats in the European Cup. Perhaps the unluckiest team during this era was the French side, St Etienne, who, playing splendid football, were supremely unlucky to lose to Bayern in Glasgow in 1976.

Now came the challenge of Liverpool.

For seven eventful seasons in the 1970s under their gregarious manager, Bill Shankly, they had won the League Championship four times, and been runners-up three times. In 1975 and 1976, they twice captured both the League title and the UEFA Cup. The supremacy at home had been gained from Leeds United, who by now without their manager, Don Revie, were faltering. Leeds managed to reach the European Cup final in 1975 against Bayern in Paris but after they fell behind to another Muller goal, the Leeds fans rioted – an ugly night which led to the Yorkshire side being banned from European soccer for three years.

Now with Liverpool in progressive form under Shankly's successor, Bob Paisley, the scene was set for probably their most memorable night in Rome in 1977 – the

Top *West Ham United registering an early British win in the Cup Winners Cup. Alan Sealey scores in the 1965 2-0 defeat of Munich 1860.*

Below *Johan Cruyff gets in a shot against Juventus in the 1973 European Cup final.*

73

opposition in the European Cup final were the West German champions, Borussia Moenchengladbach, boosted by the presence of the then European Footballer of the Year, Allan Simonsen. It was he who drove in a mighty equaliser after McDermott had put the English champions into the lead with a clever Heighway-organised goal in the first half. But on this balmy hot night in the Olympic Stadium, Kevin Keegan produced his own virtuoso show – and inspired Merseysiders to take an irrevocable lead with goals by Smith, the old fox, and a penalty by Neal.

It was a glorious night of celebration for Keegan, but not long afterwards, he was transferred to Hamburg for £500,000. A year later, with the former Celtic striker, Dalglish, in the side as Keegan's replacement, Liverpool reclaimed the major trophy by beating FC Bruges by one Dalglish goal at Wembley. And now came the turn of Nottingham Forest.

Brian Clough, with his assistant, Peter Taylor, was instrumental in urging the incredible transformation of a side long used to the backwaters of the Second Division. After promotion was gained in 1977, Forest won the Football League championship in 1978, and the European Cup twice in 1979 and 1980. The first victory against Malmo was earned from a

goal by Trevor Francis, playing in a European Cup-tie for the first time, and the second against Hamburg by an opportunist goal by John Robertson. No wonder Keegan retired to his hotel room afterwards to meditate on what might have been.

Nottingham Forest were knocked out of the 1980-81 European Cup in an early round by CSKA Sofia. But the healthy challenge thrown down by British clubs in all three European competitions continued after those faulty beginnings early on. If anything, the standards of the two other competitions, the Cup Winners Cup and the UEFA Cup, had improved considerably over the years, particularly in the UEFA Cup, which now demands a two-leg final, at home and away. In all the European competitions English clubs have enjoyed more wins than those of any other country, having passed the total of Spanish clubs, with Italian and West German clubs well behind.

The Cup Winners Cup had produced five British winners to the 1980s – the great Spurs side winning it back in 1963, West Ham, in 1965, Manchester City, in 1970, Chelsea, in 1971 and Glasgow Rangers in 1972. In the Rangers defeat of Moscow Dynamo in Barcelona, the Scots fans rioted and after ugly confrontations with the

Spanish police. Rangers were banned for a period from this competition.

Six English clubs won the old Fairs Cup and, later, the UEFA Cup before the start of the 1981-82 season – Leeds (twice), Newcastle, Arsenal, Tottenham, Liverpool (twice) and Ipswich. With the Football League still dominated by most of the teams mentioned above, plus such thriving sides as Aston Villa and a resurgent West Ham United at last reclaiming their First Division status, future English prizes in Europe surely would not be delayed for long.

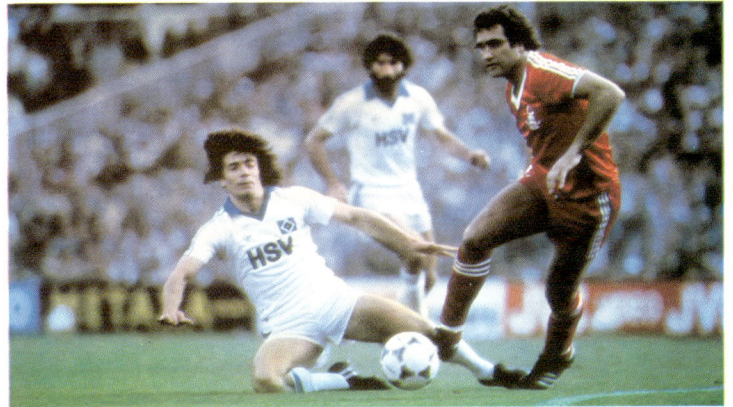

Forest retained the European Cup in 1980, when in the final against Hamburg they found Kevin Keegan, previously of Liverpool, playing against them.
Above Keegan fails to stop Larry Lloyd.
Left The only goal. Robertson (dark shirt, behind No 7) scores in the corner from just outside the box.

The World Cup
Michael Archer

FIFA, football's world governing body, started life in 1904 with seven members and a clause in its constitution saying it alone could run a World Cup competition. But it was 1928 before the idea of a championship every four years became reality. A year later Uruguay won the right to stage the first tournament. Their case was based on winning the Olympic gold medal in 1924 and 1928, their centenary being in 1930, a promise to build a new 100,000-capacity stadium *and* the promise to pay every team's full expenses. It was an offer all but 13 of FIFA's now 41-strong membership saw fit to decline.

1930 – Uruguay
The three-week sea journey was a deterrent to all but four European teams. The Home countries withdrew from FIFA in 1928 so there was no British interest. France decided to go four weeks before the start. Rumania went because King Carol picked the team! And outside Belgium and Yugoslavia, the only challenge to seven South American sides came from the U.S.A. – nicknamed the shot-putters because of their size. And with six ex-British professionals in their side they surprised Belgium and Paraguay (both 3-0) to reach the semi-finals along with Yugoslavia, who upset the seeded Brazilians 2-1. But the formbook then returned to normality. Argentina scored five in the second half against U.S.A. to win 6-1 and Uruguay recovered from being one down in four minutes to smash the Yugoslavs by the same score. So it was a repeat of the 1928 Olympic Final. Argentina were 2-1 up at half-time. But Cea dribbled through for a brilliant equaliser, Iriarte put Uruguay in front and Castro made sure with a fourth.

1934 – Italy
Uruguay declined to defend their title in 1934, and Argentina sent a team of 'reserves'. Winger Orsi had been lured to Italy before the 1930 finals and now their captain and centre half Monti had followed him. Vittorio Pozzo managed an Italian side that had to win to please Mussolini. They began by swamping U.S.A. (with only three of their 1930 team) 7-1. In the quarter-finals they faced Spain and their legendary captain and goalkeeper Zamora. Almost single-handed he took a brutal tie to a replay. Crippled by injury, and frustrated by spineless refereeing, Spain went out to a Meazza header, while Hugo Meisl's 'Wunderteam' from Austria survived a 'war' against neighbours Hungary to reach the other semi-final. But in the mud of Milan Austria succumbed to a goal from another Argentinian exile, Guaita. So Italy's last hurdle was Czechoslovakia, who emerged from their semi-final convincing 3-1 winners over Germany.

Seventy minutes – no score, then Puc returned from injury to put Czechoslovakia in front. Eight minutes from time and Orsi dipped a freak shot over Czech keeper Planicka for the equaliser . . . extra time. Now fitness told and Schiavio rifled home a shot which made it a home victory for the second time.

1938 – France
Both Uruguay *and* Argentina refused to compete, while manager Pozzo reckoned Italy stronger than in 1934. The seven first-round ties produced two replays, three decisions after extra time and 44 goals! Czechoslovakia needed extra time to beat Holland as did Italy against little Norway. Germany, under Sepp Herberger, were taken to a replay by Switzerland and then despatched 4-2. But, in the first great World Cup upset Cuba (late replacements for Mexico) held Rumania 3-3 and recovered from a goal down to win the replay 2-1. Leonidas of Brazil and Poland's Willimowski both scored four in a crazy match that ended 6-5 to Brazil.

Sweden drew a first round bye before

The big match in the 1934 World Cup was the Italy-Austria semi-final, won by this goal from Italy's Guaita in the mud of Milan.

The finalists line up before the 1938 World Cup Final in Paris as the band plays the national anthems.

Italy's goalkeeper beaten in the 1938 final, but Italy beat Hungary 4-2 to retain the trophy.

despatching Cuba 8-0. In Paris, hosts met holders and sadly for the French, Piola's two second half goals gave Italy, in their Fascist black strip, a 3-1 win. In Bordeaux meanwhile came one of the great disgraces in World Cup history . . . Czechoslovakia v Brazil. Two Brazilians and a Czech were sent off. The Czechs also lost goalkeeper Planicka with a broken arm and Nejedly (whose penalty sent the game into inconclusive extra time) with a broken leg. Brazil made nine changes for the replay and came from behind to win 2-1. But in the semi-final, they succumbed 2-1 to Italy. The final hurdle for the holders was Hungary, who annihilated Sweden 5-1 in their semi-final. Italian skipper Meazza was in decisive form creating three goals. Piola and Colaussi both scored twice as Italy triumphed again, 4-2.

1950 – Brazil

The world's biggest stadium, the 200,000-capacity Maracana in Rio de Janeiro, welcomed back the World Cup after the war. Understandably Brazil were strongly fancied. But now England, back in the FIFA fold, were there with a team that included Matthews, Finney, Mannion and Ramsey. Their 2-0 opening win over a Chile side that included Newcastle's George Robledo gave no hint of the nightmare that awaited the co-favourites in their next match. The U.S.A., a veritable jumble of nationalities, skippered by a Scot who had been given a free transfer by Third Division Wrexham, had already lost 3-1 to Spain. In Belo Horizonte they scored one goal that made history. England had no reply or excuse. Wholesale changes for the match against Spain could not disguise the 'shellshock'. Another single goal went the wrong way and England were out. Spain went through with maximum points while Chile put the U.S.A. in proper perspective with a 5-2 win.

The 'Final Pool' operated on a league system. Brazil started brilliantly. First they trounced Sweden, managed by Yorkshireman George Raynor, 7-1 with Ademir getting four, and then they saw off Spain 6-1. Their skill and understanding seemed in a class of its own. But Uruguay meanwhile had ground out a 2-2 draw with Spain and came from behind twice to beat the Swedes 3-2. So if they could beat Brazil in what was truly the final they would take the trophy. The hosts were 10-1 on favourites; a draw was all they needed to earn their £10,000 win bonuses.

Uruguay survived a first half bombardment but two minutes into the second half Friaca scored for Brazil – surely the decisive breakthrough. But a break down the right saw the unmarked Schiaffino net the equaliser, and the home crowd could not

believe it when Perez stole the winner for Uruguay eleven minutes from time.

1954 – Switzerland

Hungary looked unstoppable in 1954. Unbeaten in four years, they had destroyed England 6-3 at Wembley and 7-1 in Budapest. Ferenc Puskas 'generalled' a side of quite breathtaking talent.

They started by swamping South Korea 9-0, and then ran up against a West German side managed by the wily Sepp Herberger. Having beaten Turkey 4-1, he reasoned that he could do so again in a play-off and still qualify for the quarter-finals. He played a team of reserves against Hungary and watched Kocsis score four in the favourites' 8-3 win. What's more, Puskas was injured. The play-off went as planned – 7-2 to West Germany. England meanwhile squandered a 3-1 lead against Belgium to draw 4-4 and Scotland, appearing for the first time, succumbed to a brilliant Austrian goalkeeper and a first-half goal by Probst. Manager Andy Beattie then resigned and the Scots crashed 7-0 to Uruguay. England's 2-0 win over Switzerland saw them through to the quarter-finals but goalkeeper Merrick would want to forget Uruguay's 4-2 win. West Germany, back to full strength, were flattered by their 2-0 win over Yugoslavia. Switzerland, having twice beaten Italy in the preliminaries, faced Austria in a quarter-final, memorable for all the right reasons – 12 goals! Nine came in the first half, three in as many minutes for Austria, who won 7-5. But in Berne, all the wrong headlines with Brazil involved in another disgrace. A match of two penalties and three sendings-off ended with Hungary winning 4-2 and the fighting spilling into the dressing room. Mercifully, Hungary's semi-final win over Uruguay by the same score fully restored the good name of football, while Germany swamped Austria with five second-half goals.

So a Hungary v West Germany final and Puskas back in action. Inside eight minutes he had scored and Hungary led 2-0. Not for long. Morlock and winger Rahn scored before half time. Fifteen minutes from the end Rahn got his second – and that was enough. Hungary hit the woodwork twice and had a goal disallowed. The favourites were dead; Herberger had done it.

1958 – Sweden

All four British teams made the 1958 finals. But the world rather remembers them for Brazil and a 17-year-old known as Pelé. England, weakened by the Munich air disaster, were drawn in Brazil's group along with Olympic champions Russia, who boasted one of the game's greatest goalkeepers in Lev Yashin. So, coming

from 2-0 down to draw 2-2 was adequate against Russia; a goalless draw with Brazil (even without Pelé, Zito and Garrincha) was better still. But England went out 1-0 in a play-off with Russia after hitting the post twice. Better luck for Northern Ireland and Wales. The Irish beat Czechoslovakia 1-0, held West Germany with two McParland goals and went through by beating the Czechs again with two more from McParland in extra time. Wales' play-off was against Hungary, depleted now by the 1956 revolution. Allchurch and Medwin got the goals in an excellent 2-1 win. But Scotland bowed out, beaten by Paraguay and France.

Now it was Wales' turn against Brazil – and without big John Charles. They played superbly, containing the wily Garrincha. But a solitary Pelé goal was deflected past the brilliant Kelsey. Northern Ireland also went down – 4-0 to France.

Sweden, meanwhile, still under George Raynor, progressed smoothly to the quarter-finals, dropping only one point in a goalless draw with Wales. Home support grew with a 2-0 win over Russia, inspired by one of their Italian professional exiles, Kurt Hamrin. Now only Germany stood between them and the final.

It was a stormy semi-final. Germany's Juskowiak lost patience with Hamrin and

Above Pelé was the exciting newcomer in the 1958 World Cup. Here he is in the final challenging the Swedish goalkeeper Kalle Svensson.

Right Wales' most successful World Cup was in 1958, when they had two great players in Allchurch and John Charles, seen here heading towards the Mexican goal.

was sent off before Hamrin wrapped up a 3-1 win. In the other semi-final France were holding Brazil 1-1 at half-time. Then Didi started the rot and proceeded to lay on three more for Pelé.

At least France took third place, beating Germany 6-3, with Fontaine bringing his goals total to a record 13.

Liedholm gave Raynor and Sweden the start they wanted in the final, scoring in four minutes. But by half-time Vava had finished off two Garrincha openings. The prodigious Pelé left Sweden gasping with two more and Zagalo got the other one in a 5-2 win.

1962 – Chile

Brazil were still strong, though Pelé survived only one game. England came with new boys Bobby Moore and Bobby Charlton alongside Haynes and Greaves.

England's opener, a 2-1 defeat by Hungary, was disappointing. Better followed against Argentina. Charlton and Greaves scored in a 3-1 win. A goalless draw with Bulgaria took Britain's only representatives through on goal average. But now they faced Brazil. The holders had beaten Mexico, lost Pelé with a torn muscle in the goalless draw with Czechoslovakia and come from behind to beat Spain 2-1.

England simply could not hold the un-gainly Garrincha. He headed home a corner, unleashed a freekick that Springett could only present to Vava and then rifled home Brazil's third himself. Gerry Hitchens from Inter Milan got the England goal.

Hosts Chile beat Switzerland and then fell foul of Italy. In the most violent game of the tournament two Italians were sent off and one had his nose broken. Chile won 2-0 and went through with the Germans.

Russia survived an amazing 4-4 draw with the unfancied Colombians, after leading 3-0, and then another brutal match with the Yugoslavs which they won 2-0. Russia's quarter-final with Chile was tilted by fervent home support and goalkeeper Yashin's second poor game, leaving the Chileans to face Brazil and Garrincha. He scored two and made another in Brazil's 4-2 win which took them through to a final against the outsiders Czechoslovakia.

The sides had drawn 0-0 in the first round. Since then the Czechs had beaten Hungary 1-0 and Yugoslavia 3-1 – both wins thanks largely to goalkeeper Schroiff. But he had run out of good games.

Masopust shocked the holders with an early goal. But Amarildo squeezed one in from an impossible angle, Zito headed a second, which with Vava's decisive third goal, when Schroiff dropped Djalma Santos' cross, kept the Cup in Brazil.

The winning Brazilian side in 1962. Left to right, back: D. Santos, Zito, Gilmar, Zozimo, N. Santos, Mauro. Front: Masajista (masseur), Garincha, Didi, Vava, Amarildo, Zagalo, Asis (trainer). Pelé was injured.

1966 – England

Alf Ramsey worked miracles as manager at Ipswich and learned harsh lessons from the U.S.A. and Hungary in the 1950s. Now his England team played a new 4-3-3 system. Three world-class players and Wembley for all their matches persuaded even the inscrutable Ramsey to forecast, "We will win".

People questioned his judgement after the frustrating goalless draw with Uruguay. Where was the flair? Bobby Charlton showed a glimpse in the 2-0 win over the equally negative Mexicans, with a blistering 30-yard shot. Against France the form 'sagged'. The willing Hunt got both goals, but Stiles' foul on Herbin blemished another unconvincing performance.

Brazil started with Pelé blasting a free-kick and Garrincha a famous 'banana shot'

The end of the gallant North Koreans in 1966. Augusto heads Portugal's fifth in the quarter-final, after North Korea had been three up.

Bene, who played well for Hungary throughout the tournament, raises his arms after scoring against Russia in the 1966 quarter-final, but Russia won 2-1.

against Bulgaria. But the omens were there in the tackling. In the next match Brazil met Hungary for the first time since the 1954 'Battle of Berne'. Pelé was unfit. Thankfully skill decided the match – but Hungary's way. They were ahead in three minutes from Bene, Farkas volleyed one of the great goals of the tournament and Meszoly's penalty wrapped it up at 3-1. Portugal finally put paid to the double champions. As Pelé hobbled out of the tournament after a dreadful foul, Eusebio claimed the star billing with two goals in another 3-1 result.

Italy's exit was far more embarrassing . . . against the 'mini-men' of North Korea. Months of monastic preparation paid off and the delighted Middlesbrough crowd saw Pak Doo Ik score a goal that gave Korea a win that sent manager Fabbri and his team home in disgrace.

But the North Koreans were not finished! In the quarter-finals, they led Portugal 3-0 after 24 minutes. But Eusebio scored two in each half, including two penalties, and Portugal won 5-3. England's quarter-final was against Argentina – 'Animals', Ramsey called them after a disgraceful incident in which their captain Rattin was

sent off and refused to go for eight minutes. Hurst, replacing Greaves, headed England's winner.

Russia put out Hungary and now faced West Germany in the semi-final. Helmut Schoen's team had dispatched Switzerland 5-0, survived a goalless draw with Argentina (who had Albrecht sent off) and beaten Spain 2-1. Their challenge was underlined when they exposed the South

Below The most controversial incident of the 1966 World Cup was the sending off of Argentina's Rattin in the quarter-final against England.
Bottom The goal which finally settled it. Hurst's third and England's fourth in the 1966 final.

George Cohen, Jack Charlton, Bobby Moore and Geoff Hurst celebrate with the Cup.

American temperament again. Uruguay had two sent off and caved in 4-0. Against Russia, Germany won 2-1 – unimpressively, considering the Russians had Sabo sent off and Chislenko limping.

England's semi-final win over Portugal was a triumph for Bobby Charlton with two goals, and Stiles in midfield, who subdued Eusebio. He did score the first goal England had conceded but it was a penalty and came too late.

So Germany stand between Ramsey and his prediction.

14 minutes – a weak clearance, Haller shoots, 1-0 to Germany.

20 minutes – a Moore freekick, Hurst's header, 1-1.

78 minutes – Peters a volley, 2-1 to England ... surely the winner ... but 89 minutes – Emmerich hammers a disputed freekick and Weber finishes it off, 2-2 and extra time.

100 minutes – Ball to Hurst; the shot bounces down off the bar. The linesman says 'Goal'; the Germans will never agree.

Seconds left – Moore the clearance, Hurst gallops through, the net bulges ... 4-2. No argument now!

1970 – Mexico

England looked stronger than in 1966. But so did Brazil. Pelé at his peak now lined up with talents like Tostao, Jairzinho, Rivelinho and Gerson under new manager Zagalo. Italy were European champions. And Germany had Muller to finish off the creative work of Beckenbauer and Overath.

Hurst's goal saw England through against the brutal Rumanians; Brazil beat the Czechs 4-1 and now it was . . . England v Brazil. Ramsey was detested by the South American media; his team were kept awake at night by chanting mobs, and en route to Mexico skipper Moore had been 'framed' and imprisoned in Bogota on a ridiculous theft charge. The high altitude and the 100 degree heat did not help either. But England were superb. Their organisation was typified and inspired by Moore. Pelé's one real chance – a header – brought a save from goalkeeper Banks that will never be forgotten. But eventually Pelé set up Jairzinho for a decisive goal. England missed at least two chances to equalise.

Italy, disrupted by internal rows, scraped through 1-0 against Sweden and were then held 0-0 by both Uruguay and little Israel. The quarter-final against Mexico gave signs of better things. Riva scored two, and Rivera's introduction for the second half produced a 4-1 result.

England's quarter-final was against the old enemy, West Germany, who had survived an early shock to beat Morocco and then disposed of Bulgaria 5-2 and the exciting Peruvians (managed by Didi) 3-1, with hat-tricks for Muller.

In the second half, England led 2-0 with goals from Mullery and Peters. It looked all over when Ramsey decided to substitute Peters and Bobby Charlton (his last international appearance). But first Beckenbauer's shot beat the dive of Bonetti, who had replaced the sick Banks. Then the veteran Seeler (his fourth World Cup) back-headed a freak goal through Bonetti's hands . . . 2-2 and extra time. In it, Grabowski (a telling substitution by Schoen) crossed to the far post, Lohr headed back and Muller completed England's misery with the winning volley.

The Germans also faced extra time in the semi-final against Italy. Schnellinger it was who got their equaliser in injury time. But their hopes vanished with a shoulder injury to Beckenbauer and although Muller scored twice, Rivera climaxed an amazing match with Italy's winner.

Brazil, having tamed the bubbling Peruvians, now faced Uruguay who had beaten Russia with a single disputed goal in extra time. There was no disputing Brazil's superiority in a 3-1 win even though Uruguay led until just before half-time.

And there was no argument about

Brazil's mastery in the final. Pelé opened the scoring in his World Cup finale and laid on another for Jairzinho. Gerson and skipper Carlos Alberto got the other goals. Brazil 4, Italy 1. Their third win gave Brazil the Jules Rimet trophy to keep.

1974 – West Germany

Brazil were in decline – Pelé had gone. England, having to qualify for the first time since 1962, had been pipped at the post by Poland. Scotland carried the British banner but were blighted by disputes over commercial ventures and team discipline. Germany were hot favourites with Bayern Munich the new European champions (and providing six of the squad) not to mention the Olympic Stadium venue for the final and the guiding influence of skipper 'Kaiser' Franz Beckenbauer.

West Germany scraped home 1-0 against Chile, had some uneasy moments against the 'Socceroos' from Australia before winning 3-0, and then faced their Communist neighbours from East Germany. Security was fantastic, police were everywhere. But the formbook failed – on and off the pitch. No riots or terrorism and East Germany won! Sparwasser got the only goal of the game and significantly it meant that East not West Germany faced the Dutch in the second round.

The contrast was Scotland. The only unbeaten side in the tournament was eliminated. Their misfortune was opening against Zaire and only winning 2-0. Goal

difference was decisive this time. So with Brazil beating the Africans 3-0 and Yugoslavia 9-0, draws with both Brazil and Yugoslavia were not enough for Willie Ormond's team.

Italy began as if 1966 would repeat itself. Haiti scored the first goal against them in 13 games but the Latins recovered their composure to win 3-1. Against Argentina only a silly own goal earned them a 1-1 draw and then they faced Poland – who, even without star striker Lubanski, had beaten Argentina 3-2 and Haiti 7-0. The Poles won with glorious goals from Szarmach and Deyna.

Holland, meanwhile, always inspired by Cruyff, had despatched Uruguay 2-0 with two Rep goals; drawn 0-0 with Sweden

Opposite above *West Germany's penalty in the 1974 final, slotted home by Paul Breitner.*

Opposite below *Argentina's final and settling goal in the 1978 final, being scored by Bertoni.*

and overrun Bulgaria 4-1. Now they showed their real class. Argentina were swept aside 4-0, with Cruyff scoring twice. The East Germans put a man on Cruyff but it did not prevent Neeskens and Rensenbrink getting the decisive goals ... which left Brazil in Holland's path. The new artists needed only a draw against the old. How disappointing that, with Jairzinho and Rivelino still playing, the South Americans resorted to violence. Pereira was sent off as thrilling goals by Cruyff and Neeskens sent Holland through to the final.

1978 – Argentina

Home advantage was again decisive, though in fairness to manager Menotti Argentina's blend of South American skill with European pace would have taken some stopping even without the ticker-tape frenzy of fans in the River Plate Stadium.

England missed out on goal difference to Italy. So British eyes were on Scotland. Manager Ally MacLeod told the world they could win, despite failing to do so in the recent Home Internationals. Again self-destruction swamped self-belief. There

An aerial save from Yugoslavia's goalkeeper Maric, while Jordan is prevented from interfering in the 1974 finals. Scotland were eliminated without losing a match.

Similarly, West Germany, needing only a draw on the rain-sodden pitch in Frankfurt against Poland, missed a penalty but won with a Muller goal.

The final began amazingly. Holland kicked off and, in 15 unbroken passes, Cruyff was chopped down for a penalty. Neeskens scored. But the Germans equalised from another penalty and Muller snapped up what turned out to be the winner, before half-time. West Germany survived a terrific second half siege to emulate Herberger's 1954 side – losing a battle to win a war.

were wrangles over fees and bonuses and, after a disastrous start, winger Johnston was sent home following a positive dope test. Scotland led against Peru but Cubillas flighted home a deceptive freekick, Masson missed a penalty, and the Scots lost 3-1. Worse followed against Iran. Only a silly own goal gave them a 1-1 draw. Now they must beat the formidable Dutch by three goals. At last they played to their potential. The diminutive Gemmill scored twice (including one of the cleverest goals of the tournament) but 3-2 was not enough, even though it was Holland's only defeat before

Argentina's marauding attackers, Luque, Kempes and Bertoni, celebrating during the 1978 final.

They knew the exact target because of their later kick-off time than Brazil, who beat Poland 3-1. The cynics smiled before – and particularly after – Argentina hit six past Peru's Argentine-born goalkeeper Quiroga.

The final was another 'might have been' for Holland. Man-of-the-match (and the tournament) Kempes scored for Argentina after 38 minutes. Holland only equalised through substitute Nanninga eight minutes from time. Yet, right on the whistle, Rensenbrink hit a post. In extra time, Kempes struck again and set up a third for Bertoni. For the third time in four World Cups, the host nation celebrated.

Uruguay 1980-81

The 'Little World Cup', the Copa de Oro tournament from December 30 1980 to January 10 1981 completed the 50-year 'cycle'. Uruguay staged a tournament of all the champions. Only England was missing, unable to release players in the middle of a League season. In their place went Holland. Europe v South America proved an emphatic triumph for the latter. Uruguay, who assembled two months in advance, were too strong for both Holland and Italy – literally in the latter case. Italy's Cabrini and Tardelli and Moreira of Uruguay were sent off. A Morales penalty helped Uruguay to win again 2-0.

In the other group, Germany were also eclipsed. Against Argentina they did manage to subdue the brilliant Maradona and, in fact, led by a Hrubesch goal until five minutes from time. Then Passarella equalised and Diaz got the winner.

Argentina failed for the eighth time under Menotti to beat Brazil. Maradona scored spectacularly against the run of play but defender Edevaldo earned Brazil a draw. So Brazil needed a two-goal win over West Germany to make the final. The Germans, despite losing Kaltz, led with an Allofs goal until the 58th minute when they caved in to lose 4-1.

So Uruguay v Brazil for the Gold Cup – the 50th meeting in full internationals, a match kicked off by Mascheroni, a winner with Uruguay in 1930 and the only survivor. He had his happy ending too. Substitute Barrios scored in 50 minutes and Socrates' penalty made absolutely sure, even though Victorino got a late goal for Brazil. The winners celebrated in the Centenario Stadium's moat!

the final. Scotland went out, again, on goal difference.

France opened with a Lacombe goal in 31 seconds against Italy, yet were eliminated by an absurd penalty conceded by defender Tresor against Argentina. If Passarella had missed it, Argentina could well have gone out on goal difference. As it was, Luque's winner came near the end. Italy, a far more adventurous side under Bearzot, actually beat Argentina with one superb Rossi-Bettega strike.

West Germany were a disappointment. They started with the fourth consecutive goalless opening match (against Poland), won only one of six games (6-0 against Mexico) and failed to score in three. Holland, having stuttered through the first round, came into their own at last. Their 5-1 win over Austria was worth an extra point and a 2-2 draw with West Germany made up for Munich in 1974.

Haan's 30-yard thunderbolt goal was a highlight of the tournament but he bettered it with a fantastic late winner against Italy which took Holland to the final again.

After Brazil and Argentina had drawn a brutal match 0-0, Argentina were left to beat Peru by four goals to get there too.

Soccer Today:
A Biased Footballer's View
Steve Coppell

For a long time now one has only to turn to the back pages of any newspaper or switch on the television, to be bombarded by the thoughts of the game's analysts, all unanimously predicting that the downfall of football in Britain is imminent. We are told that like a lot of industry in Britain today, football is living in the past. It has not grown to meet the demands of the modern society, so it, like many staple industries, will inevitably fall.

But let us be realistic. Surely football has faced and overcome such crises before? The economic climate of the 1920s was undoubtedly more severe than the situation today. In the 1920s the value of football was such that housewives always tried to have enough spare cash to send their man to the football. This outlet enabled many clubs to establish their record attendances in the late 1920s and early 1930s. Although there is now much more leisure competition for any spare cash that is available, football is so embedded in the lives of most of the male population that there is little chance that it will be allowed to shrivel up and die.

In fact the only people to gain from the daily knock at football are this growing army of analysts who have realised that it is easy and profitable to criticise. A reflection on the strength and character within English football should hopefully put an end to this new parasitic sector and guarantee that the poison pens run dry.

When one looks idealistically at football today there is a need for change, or growth as I prefer to call such action, but the condition is not so critical as to demand wholesale panic.

An outsider's view of English football is reflected in the standard of our national side, and at the moment we cannot be ranked very highly. After England's poor performance in the 1980 European Championships in Italy there cannot be too many people who think we have much chance of doing well in the 1982 World Cup finals in Spain. But the British bulldog is a fighting breed and I feel British football in general will be well represented by any of the four home nations who go to Spain. England's qualification, though taken for granted by many, is a long way from being a foregone conclusion. Their defeat in Rumania made sure of that. As a biased player, I am confident that we will see an England team among the 24 who play-off in Spain.

A by-product of the defeat in Rumania was the concrete realisation that international football comes a poor second to club football in England. The national team was unsettled by injuries to several key players sustained in the club matches the previous weekend. In most other countries the club games involving international players are suspended the week before World Cup games. Now I am not condemning this system, I am just stating the obvious: that England followers must take these problems into account when attacking Ron Greenwood or any team he picks.

By the same standards English club football remains the most entertaining in Europe, and despite our falling attendances, football in this country is envied and respected by the rest of the world. It is also successful, as for the fourth year the European Cup remained within these shores, Nottingham Forest matching the double Liverpool achieved before them. Liverpool, however, remain the standard-bearers, having been a dominant force in European football for the past fifteen years. Their football at the time of their second European Cup win led Claudio Coutinho, then manager of Brazil and Miljan Miljanic, the mentor of Cruyff, to say that if Liverpool were allowed to enter the World Cup, then they would undoubtedly finish in the first three. This statement speaks volumes in defence of a supposedly ailing football nation.

Liverpool and Forest have proved that

British football can compete with and beat the best in Europe. It only remains for the international team to confirm that the traditional virtues of strength of character and aerial supremacy can overcome the technical brilliance of the Europeans and South Americans.

It is a statistical fact that the most 'entertaining' league in the world has in the past decade lost nearly six million paying spectators. The reasons for this are numerous, with different groups within the game blaming each other. Without doubt the quality of the product, ie the game, has suffered. The players blame the tactics-conscious coaches and managers, who in turn have to be successful to satisfy directors, who seem to feel the sharp edge of everyone's tongue.

I will echo my previous words in saying that I feel that the media, too, should shoulder some responsibility. Football and the press need each other; they should not abuse each other. The pessimistic speculations and doom-laden crystal-ball gazing do little to help the game.

The great majority of journalists report the facts as they appear, and one fact which is obvious to all people, and which is rightly highlighted by the media, is that the festering disease of hooliganism needs stamping out for good. I meet and talk with people who have given up their season tickets, with parents who will not let their children go to the game, or even go to the game with

A difficult problem for soccer is the disease of hooliganism.
Top *Scottish fans on the rampage after the England versus Scotland international in 1977.*
Above *English fans in Turin to watch the 1980 European Championship where tear gas was used.*
Right *Play continues during a Rangers versus Celtic match while police move in to trouble on the terraces.*

Opposite above *Steve Coppell playing for Manchester United.*
Opposite below *David Johnson playing for Liverpool and Hitachi.*

90

them, for fear of meeting up with the mindless minority who call themselves football supporters.

I have no answer to solve the problems of these misfits of modern society, but everyone must be tempted to bring back the penal establishments and sentences of years gone by to suit their particular needs.

Another reason for the attendance decline is the newly acquired awareness of the general public. Football is now in a very competitive leisure industry. From the 1920s to the 1960s, football and racing were the two main combatants for spare time, with cricket making a seasonal variation. Now games such as squash, tennis, jogging and golf are socially fashionable and well within the financial reach of most people. Leisure centres and health clubs have sprung up everywhere, so it is not really surprising that gates have fallen since the heyday of the late 1960s. Probably the only surprise is that they have not fallen by more, another acknowledgement of the place football still holds in the public's imagination, despite the many counter-attractions.

The emergence of leisure centres and the falling gates have forced clubs to realise that spectators will no longer put up with poor facilities in football grounds, and improvements have been made. Many clubs have responded to the 'centre' trend by incorporating other sports activities into their stadium complexes. But financial restraints obviously limit ambitious ground redevelopment plans. Most recently Wolves, who have started the complete rebuilding of their ground, have had to delay their plans in deference to the economic climate. Yet to a fan who watches football week in, week out and suffers all the vagaries of the weather on unprotected terraces, it seems unfair for him to have to eat plastic food, drink lukewarm powdered tea and put up with unhygienic toilet facilities, while his chairman is seen chomping on an Havana, sipping champagne and signing a £1 million-plus player. The logic is distinctly Irish.

By all conventional economic meters, football is in a financial rut which is fast becoming a grave for some clubs. A couple of years back the total debt of Football League clubs was estimated to be £19 million. The unawareness of the need to be frugal which is evident throughout football is perhaps best typified with Manchester

City and Steve Daly. Steve was bought for £1·5 million, yet City, eighteen months later, were willing to accept £400,000 for him. Would any other industry be prepared to accept such a huge loss? I think not. The hire-purchase type of payment and over-generous bank managers mean that football, being a 'unique' industry, can overcome these losses. But surely such money could also be 'created' to complete such ventures as at Wolves and countless other venues in the country.

Everybody has now accepted that cash from the turnstiles cannot alone run a football club. Outside sources of revenue are a necessity. My own club, Manchester United, though blessed with the highest gates in the country, still needs the assistance of a thankfully thriving Development Association, which raises cash by lotteries, etc. Nearly all clubs have similar organisations which subsidise the football activities. United have also had the foresight to build a restaurant and conference facilities on site, and as at many grounds there are executive boxes which cater for the needs of the privileged few. The future seems to lie in this direction, with clubs trying to make their grounds a focal point of community attention.

Many clubs also see a big future in linking with a major chain store or multiple group. The leaders in this field are Aston Villa who have an ASDA superstore built next to the ground, along with a gymnasium complex. Everyone benefits from this type of arrangement, and other clubs have been quick to see the possibilities, notably Millwall, who have taken the idea a stage further. They planned to start work at the end of the 1980-81 season with a development which again involves ASDA but also the local council in Lewisham. Because of this three-way co-operation the community should, in three years time, have a new ground, leisure complex and superstore all grouped together. The active participation of the local council could set an example to other councils, who have been understandably wary of such gambles in view of the government's restrictions on local authority spending. If it proves to be a success, football clubs could be freed from the crippling overhead costs of decaying grounds. Most stadiums on the Continent and in America are owned by local authorities, and although they cater for a wide range of sports, not just one, they are more

modern and invariably better cared for. People feel a community pride in these complexes and look after the facilities, whereas in this country the buildings are more often used as the backdrops for the local graffiti artists.

Immediately following on from this source of revenue comes sponsorship. We have already seen the introduction of advertising on a number of teams' strips in Britain, yet the reported cash involvement, even for prestige-laden Liverpool, does not compare with the amounts paid to European clubs. This is because teams there can wear shirts bearing the sponsors' name during televised games. Legislation in England does not at present cater for this, as football suffers from the double-edged values that exist in the sporting and television world. For example, racing cars are daubed with sponsors' names on every available inch of space, and in show-jumping, horses are renamed to meet the demands of sponsors. In fact, most other televised sport contravenes the standards set for televising football. Until shirt advertising is allowed on television, income will be slipping through the clubs' fingers, and when the television contract next comes up for negotiation this aspect will have to be clarified.

Television in general is a very touchy subject. Football has lost almost six million paying spectators in the last decade, yet this figure has been more than doubly compensated for by larger television audiences watching football. Every weekend there is a nucleus of approximately thirteen million people watching football on ITV and BBC. Who can blame people for viewing at home when there is now a goal coverage of at least seven games each weekend. This must affect those marginal spectators who occasionally go, but more often do not, 'because it's bound to be on the box anyway'.

I am as big a football fan as anybody, but I think the saturation coverage we have for nine months of the year spoils even the 'live' spectator on a Saturday into expecting action replays. I would expect that unless the television companies make the football clubs an offer they cannot refuse, there will be less football on TV in years to come.

As football entered the 1980s the hysteria created by the scandal-mongers has meant that any organisation or body connected with football, has had a 'crisis'

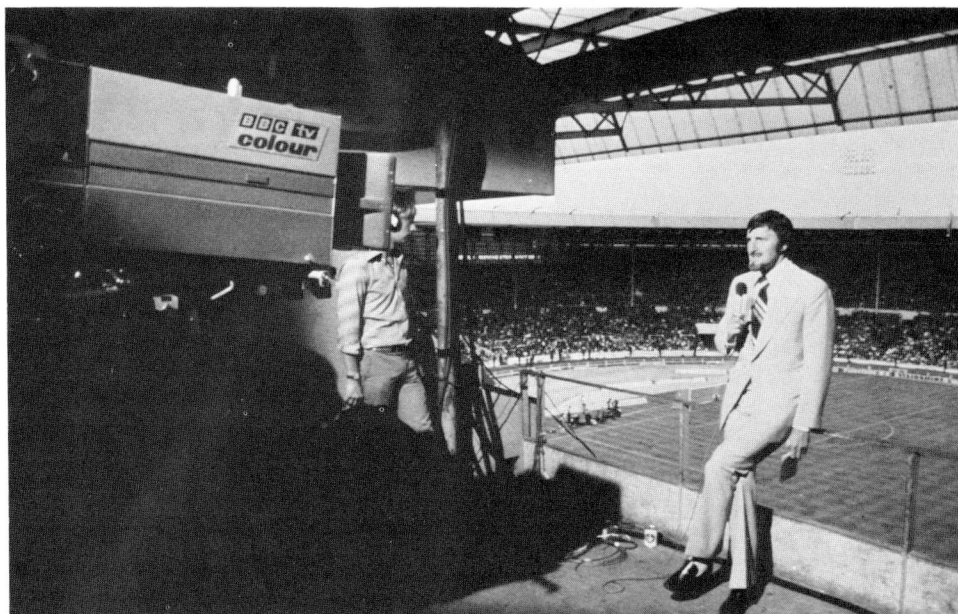

meeting to discuss ways of injecting new life into the national game. The Football League, the Football Association, the League chairmen, the secretaries, managers, coaches and physiotherapists, the PFA . . . all seem to have proposals with the caring of the game as their objective. In the main these ideas run roughly along the same lines, but legislative change will be slow due to the large number of governing bodies involved. The game is moving forward to the same destination via five or six different routes, and this is hardly the most efficient navigation system.

The government recognised this root problem and in its 1979 'Royal Commission on Gambling' suggested the introduction of a ruling Football Board, which initially would redirect a portion of the pools profits to much needed areas. This Board under the auspices of a previously detached chairman would hopefully put an end to the power struggle that exists within English football. But, like many government white papers, this has apparently been left to gather dust on the shelf and the pools companies and the governing bodies concerned have all heaved a sigh of relief.

Cricket, that doyen of conservatism and tradition, in the late 1970s underwent so great a metamorphosis that women are now allowed in the Long Room at Lord's. More importantly, the game has risen, Phoenix-like, from the ashes (sorry!) of boring three-day activity, to the intense

thrills and showmanship of instant cricket. The catalyst of this reaction came in the form of a dour Australian called Kerry Packer, who changed more in a decade than had previously changed in a century. Football too has found a Kerry Packer, but in the form of a massive land mass known as North America. Despite several promptings and false alarms, it seems as if soccer has at last taken root, and is even spreading its branches. No longer is American football the last lucrative stop-off for retiring footballers, it is now a voracious monster fast outgrowing its parents.

Commercially, the Americans superbly gift-wrap a poor product, but the quality of the product is improving, and a generation of Americans brought up on a regular diet of soccer will one day make the country a force in World Cup football. I myself received a letter from a young American boy who religiously practices five hours a day to perfect his ball skills, and he was asking me for tips!

Such typical American energy is even more evident in the promotion of American soccer games, with their enthusiastic crowds responding wholeheartedly to the players who arrive on the pitch on or in every conceivable form of transport from elephants to helicopters. This makes for a great spectacle and as soccer is one of the few sports in that country to have increasing attendances, there is a movement in Britain to copy their presentation. Indeed a start has been made with many clubs

The American scene. The two-tier R.F.K. Stadium in Washington.

Below *Stadiums need not be lacking all but the most primitive facilities, as so many are in Britain. Fans have escalators to take them to their seats in this American stadium.*

installing the electric scoreboards and employing girl cheerleaders. I personally feel it could be wrong to go much further. I would not really imagine Trafford Park on a raw January morning with rows of estate cars being used for barbecues and picnics.

Just to accentuate the point further, a couple of years ago United played against Tampa Bay Rowdies in an exhibition match. Now Tampa is one of the more conservative American clubs, but unfortunately their supporters are nicknamed 'fannies'. On the day of our game the club were running a 'Best Dressed Granny Fanny' competition. This amounted to an assortment of shapes, sizes and ages all wearing the club colours of bright yellow and green from head to toe! One could hardly imagine such a competition being a success in Manchester or Liverpool.

America has served its 'Kerry Packer' purpose. It has made the English game look at itself, and the snowball effect is still continuing with clubs wanting to improve all the time. Because of different climates and more importantly different mentalities, the British can never mirror the American approach, but we are refining some of their better ideas to suit our game.

Football today is at a crossroads, and who is to say which road we will find ourselves on?

Certainly not me. But as an economist who views most things in terms of peaks and troughs, I would say that after a depression, English football is now just beginning a very gentle upswing. In fact on a world scale, at a time when vast new areas such as America, Africa, the Middle and Far East are all at once adopting football, the horizon is distinctly sunny.

American soccer matches are often the excuse for a day out for families like these New York Cosmos fans.

Tampa Bay Rowdies cheerleaders make an avenue for players to run on to the pitch, announced by the public address and the scoreboard. This is slick American packaging at its best.